ENDORSE

Hayley Braun has been a daughter to me for over a decade. She has led with a surrendered heart and relentless fire to see a generation experience the transformative Presence of God. I count it an immense privilege to have witnessed the marking encounter with the Holy Spirit she had in 2020. The way in which Hayley has stewarded her encounter in the pages of *Surrendered to the Holy Spirit*, will mark a generation's pursuit of God and move you to yield to the next great move of God.

Kris Vallotton
Senior Associate Leader, Bethel Church, Redding, CA
Co-Founder of Bethel School of Supernatural Ministry
Author of fifteen books, including *The Supernatural Ways of Royalty*,
Spiritual Intelligence, and *Uprising*

Surrendered to Holy Spirit is one of the most important books of our time. Authored by one of the purest prophetic voices alive today. Hayley Braun is a woman consumed by the love of Jesus. Her vulnerability and humility allow us inside her beautiful, powerful relationship with Holy Spirit. Her life provides us with hope for what is possible for each one of us.

As you journey through the pages of this profound book you will find yourself yearning for more of Jesus' presence and you will feel the longing of His heart; to be known by you.

Liz Wright
Bestselling author speaker, and host of
"Live Your Best Life with Liz Wright"
CEO and Founder, International Mentoring Community

When asked who he was, John the Baptist confidently replied, "I am The voice of one crying in the wilderness: Make straight the way of the Lord." I believe God has raised up Hayley Braun as a voice in the wilderness of this hour to prepare the way for a generation to encounter the Holy Spirit.

Surrendered to the Holy Spirit is not just a book, but a call for all those hungering for a deeper experience of God. With a deep scriptural foundation and real-life experience, Hayley shows us what is not only available but what is essential for the life of every believer—a life surrendered to the person of the Holy Spirit.

Banning Liebscher
Founder, Jesus Culture

Surrendered to the Holy Spirit by Hayley Braun is a gift to the body of Christ for such a time as this. Hayley has beautifully scribed the heart and wisdom of the Lord for this hour in the heralding call from His heart drawing His people into deeper communion with the Holy Spirit and living lives of deep surrender unto Him. This book is an incredible feast table of richness of revelation that is flowing from His heart through Hayley sharing her personal encounters with the reader and wisdom He has given her. This book will give you prophetic insight, practical keys, and wisdom in the positioning for the new era—surrender. The fire of His presence and love upon these pages will ignite deeper hunger within you to know Him and I truly believe that this book is a well of encounter with Jesus that will bring healing, deliverance, alignment, awakening, strengthening and impartation. You cannot read this book and not be marked by Him. The weight this book carries comes from one who is a laid down lover of Jesus, one who is ALL IN, a friend of God, pursuing Him and has their ear upon His chest, listening to His heart and living with such tenderness toward Him, releasing the pure word of the

Lord with great authority. That is Hayley. Get ready to be marked by the fire of His presence contained in these pages.

Lana Vawser
Author and prophetic voice featured on The Elijah List,
The Australian Prophetic Council, and in Charisma Magazine

Hayley Braun is a provocation and a sign to our generation. She points the way to a passionate pursuit of Jesus and provokes us to expect more, right now, of how God wants to move on the face of the earth. This book is not simply the chronicling of an encounter with Jesus but it is a road map to its readers in unlocking ongoing encounters with Jesus for the sake of a nation, a generation and the ongoing witness of the Spirit on the earth today. In her book *Surrendered to the Holy Spirit,* she gives us a desire for the wine and the wineskin so that we as the people of God will steward his moving amongst us well. Read it, be reformed and prepared for what God is doing on the earth today!

Julian Adams
author of *Terra Nova: Your call to Redeem the Earth*
and *Make All Things New,*
founding pastor of The Table Church Boston,
and internationally recognized prophet.
founder of Vox Dei School and The Prophets Collective.

Jesus is everything, but there is no way to rightly see Him or know Him apart from the Precious Holy Spirit. Christ and Him crucified is a beauty that flesh cannot see. But, Christ and Him crucified is the beauty we *must* see. Only the Holy Spirit can make a heart *that* tender and *that* pure, because He *is* God. He *is* tenderness. He *is* purity. It is He who stirs in us first love for Jesus and fills our lamps with the oil of intimacy. The One who reveals secrets in the secret place! Oh, how we *need* The Precious

Holy Ghost. Oh, that we would learn to love Him, care for Him, and yield completely to Him!

I've known Hayley since 2008. We met the first week of BSSM during worship one day, and I think our spirit wombs leapt inside of us! I'm grateful to say that we've lived under the same roof, laughed and loved, wept and worshipped through many seasons of the spirit and soul.

I'm in tears as I type, because I've been blessed to know her up close, and I can testify of the oil. Hayley is a true friend of God, and He has trusted her with His Word for this hour.

Steffany Gretzinger
Worship Leader
Grammy Award-nominated recording artist

The message of Hayley's life is strong, real and pure. There are people that become dear trusted friends who you would trust with your life, and this girl is one of them. I'm so proud of her and this book that is a testimony of her walk with Jesus.

Jenn Johnson
Worship pastor, Bethel Church
Co-founder, Bethel Music

Hayley Braun carries a timely message for the church with prophetic insight for the present as well as truth that will keep us burning far into the future. In a world that's competing for our attention and affection, Hayley shares the beauty and importance of fixing our eyes on Jesus and seeking Him alone. I'm so happy she wrote this book and can't wait for it to be in the hands of believers everywhere!

Havilah Cunnington
Founder of Truth to Table

SURRENDERED TO THE
HOLY SPIRIT

A LIFE SATURATED
BY THE PRESENCE OF GOD

HAYLEY BRAUN

Take note that the name satan and related names are not capitalized. We choose not to acknowledge him, even to the point of violating grammatical rules.

DESTINY IMAGE® PUBLISHERS, INC.
P.O. Box 310, Shippensburg, PA 17257-0310

"Publishing cutting-edge prophetic resources to supernaturally empower the body of Christ"

This book and all other Destiny Image and Destiny Image Fiction books are available at Christian bookstores and distributors worldwide.

For more information on foreign distributors, call 717-532-3040.

Reach us on the Internet: www.destinyimage.com.

ISBN 13 TP: 978-0-7684-7371-1

ISBN 13 eBook: 978-0-7684-7356-8

For Worldwide Distribution, Printed in the USA

1 2 3 4 5 6 7 8 / 27 26 25 24 23

CONTENTS

FOREWORD

Hayley Braun, a spiritual daughter of our church family, spoke at one of our most recent conferences. She gave one of the best messages on *the gospel* I've ever heard. If not *the* best. I was amazed. Not surprised, as if such insight from her were unusual. It isn't. What surprised me was the significant rate at which her insights continue to grow, as well as how good she was at communicating such profound truths. I was deeply moved.

The Bible says to "taste and see that the Lord is good." *Taste* is experience. *See* is perception. What we experience in God will always affect what and how we see. And lest you think such encounters are dangerous, it's the absence of encounters we should fear the most. Case in point: What would the apostle Paul's ministry have been like without his Damascus Road experience? The Bible is one big storybook about the lives of people who encountered God and what they were like following that experience. Encountering God changes everything, as it should. But as true sons and daughters of God, we must value the simple as well as the overwhelming.

This book was inspired by a profound encounter Hayley had with the Lord just a few years ago. I, along with many of our team, had a front-row seat, sitting in wonder at what God was and still is doing in the heart of this treasured one. And now, countless people are being impacted by her story. She has inspired a generation to seek God first—not just an experience—but truly, seek the heart of a loving Father, whose goodness is beyond all we could have the faith or intelligence to ask for. Testimonies of God encounters have that effect.

This walk with Christ is a relational journey. It is often built up through our faithfulness in the simple moments of our lives, i.e., the daily reading of Scripture, prayer and worship in our homes, and taking time to show love and care to another. Everything along this journey is to be treasured. But it would also be irresponsible for me to imply that such overwhelming kinds of encounters with God are only for the spiritual giants of our day. It would be more correct to say that it is often the life-changing encounter that makes the spiritual giant. The point is, every one of us can and should pursue the Lord with all of our hearts, trusting Him to lead us into the kinds of experiences that best enable us to represent Him well, in a way that He receives the glory.

I have had several different moments where God touched me in life-changing ways. It has happened through the reading of Scripture, as in that moment when the Lord spoke to me out of Isaiah 60, on a Thursday afternoon in May of 1979. It has also happened as someone was teaching the Word in such a way that I knew what was being shared would change the rest of my life.

That's what happened to me when I heard my dad teach out of Ezekiel about the ministry to the Lord in the inner court, versus ministering only to the people in the outer court. I bowed my head and committed the rest of my life to learning this one thing. His teaching had that deep of an effect on me. The year was 1972. But I also remember an encounter I had with the Lord in October of 1995 that lasted all night. It was more of the overwhelming kind that I had no grid for. But it changed me.

These experiences are real and necessary. Tragically, many without such encounters teach against them. When I married my wife in 1973, it wasn't to illustrate the theology of marriage. I married her to know her, encounter her, and learn to do life with her. Should we expect anything less when we give ourselves to the lover of our souls? I think not. And so, I limit the level of influence a person has in my life if I perceive that they are satisfied with lack. But don't seek the experience. Seek Him.

Every encounter with God is an invitation to know Him. We see Moses' prayer in Exodus 33:13, "Show me your *ways* that I may know *you*." (emphasis added). Whenever the Lord unveils a part of His nature, it always comes with an invitation to encounter Him more deeply. The discovery of His heart, nature, and covenant is the great adventure we are all a part of.

Encountering God enables us to live with such an awareness of His heart and His presence that our instinctive response is to obey. In fact, the most natural response of a believer living in connection with God is to move in obedience. Great faith does not come by striving—it is the result of surrender. Our yieldedness to the Holy Spirit is what helps us to live in our divine purpose. In this way of living, it becomes natural for us to illustrate John 15:7, "Abide in Me, and let My Word abide in you, and you will ask what you will, and it will be done for you." Living in the felt realization of His presence, with His Word filling our hearts, is a natural outcome of encountering Him. The result is that we become effective by praying for things that matter to Him, and the impossibilities of life bow to the name of Jesus through our lips.

Hayley Braun is one such individual who passionately burns for the power and presence of God in the way I have described above. She has been a valuable part of our leadership team for years, overseeing various parts of the ministry school and the church. But I have had the personal privilege of watching her journey of absolute surrender to the working of the Holy Spirit in her life. This encounter has brought forth an absolute boldness, a sharp prophetic gifting, and an anointing like never before.

I am so excited about this book. There is a great impartation available for every reader. But don't just take it as a good story. Revelation 19:10 declares to us that "the testimony of Jesus is the spirit of prophecy." In other words, what He's done in one speaks of what He wants to do in another. I encourage you to allow the teaching and stories in these pages to draw you into a greater hunger and surrender to the Holy Spirit.

Bill Johnson
Bethel Church, Redding, CA
Author of *Open Heavens* and *Defining Moments*

FOREWORD

"And I will put enmity (open hostility) Between you and the woman And between your seed (offspring) and her Seed; He shall [fatally] bruise your head, And you shall [only] bruise His heel" (Genesis 3:15 AMP).

Mankind chose another tree. Eve took her attention off the Living Word of God, who walked with her in the cool of the day. The turning away from the Tree of Life, to entertain another conversation with serpent, became a doorway into apostasy. Adam and Eve feasted on another fruit and the greatest of tragedies ensued. Death became man's portion and the glory departed. However, the Father had another plan in His heart before the foundations of the world. The great Gospel of Jesus was announced and it first flowed from the mouth of God Himself. The Father preached the first Gospel message and how glorious it is. He told the serpent that a Man was coming who would crush His head, through His very own bruising. Thus, the strategy of the humble King was released. By death, God would trample death. What a mystery and what glory. Today, the message remains and it is the only message of Heaven. The message is simple, "For I determined to know nothing among you except Jesus Christ, and Him crucified" (1 Corinthians 2:2 New King James Version).

Today, firebrands like Hayley are sharing this Gospel with all who will listen. Such an arrival cannot be achieved by human effort. No, it is only experienced when the precious Holy Spirit begins to touch us and teach about Jesus. After all, this is His great pleasure. The Holy Spirit loves showing us who Jesus is. There is simply one way to know the Father and that is through Jesus. There is just one way to know Jesus and that is through the Spirit. Our experience with the beautiful Person of the Spirit is our very lifeline to the Lord of Heaven. This is why I am excited about this book. We must have more lovers of Jesus who are intimately fellowshipping with the Holy Spirit.

Hayley Braun is a blessing to us all. I believe she is after the "one thing" and the "only thing." She is shouting from the rooftops that we must all return to Jesus, the One who crushed the serpent by hanging on the cross. It is only right that she shares the Scriptures with us and tells all who will listen that we must walk in deep fellowship with the third Person of the Holy Trinity. May a generation burn to know the God-Man from Galilee, who has promised to be with us by His Spirit.

Michael Koulianos
International evangelist, conference speaker, and author
Founder, Jesus Image

CHAPTER 1

MY ENCOUNTER

WHERE IT BEGAN

On the evening of October 2019, after feeding my precious family and getting our two small children to bed, I slipped in late to our Open Heavens Conference at Bethel. I knew Michael Koulianos was ministering for our final night of the conference, and I anticipated that the Lord would move powerfully that night.

We as a family had been through a wilderness season, and I in particular had faced immense physical and emotional hardship for nearly two years.

I had been under Michael's ministry a few times, and we had some brief connection in the time that he had lived in Redding. What God was doing in his life was evident, and I was in need of a touch from the Lord.

Michael ministered to many that night, calling out people from the audience and prophesying over them. At one point, he called out people from Singapore, not realizing that a large group of them had flown out, and he ministered to each of them one by one on the stage. As Michael prayed and prophesied, it seemed as though each person he ministered to was touched powerfully by God. He started calling words of knowledge, people were getting healed, and God was there. It was getting late, and you could tell Michael was winding down when he suddenly called out my name. "Hayley Braun, get up here, Prophetess," he said. "Your face flashed in front of me." As I approached him on the stage, with most of my friends and spiritual fathers watching, he asked me, "Are you willing to prophesy if people don't like it?" Feeling the fire of God course through my body, I tried to nod and went down in the spirit. Michael began to prophesy over my voice and declared over me that the fear of man was going to die.

IT WOULD HAVE TO BE A MIRACLE

There are moments when you receive a touch from God while your mind isn't present, and there are moments when you can think and comprehend. Though I was experiencing deep emotion and feeling the presence of the Holy Spirit powerfully, my mind was present. I remember thinking while lying on the floor that night, "God, this will be a miracle if You do it; if You kill the fear of man in me, God, that will be a miracle." You see, very few people would have known that I had been wrestling with the fear of man my whole Christian walk. I had been serving in ministry since I was twelve years old and deeply loved Jesus from a young age. At the Methodist church where my parents have served for nearly fifty years, I would often get up on stage and share things the Lord was speaking to my heart or lead our congregation in passionate praise and worship. Though I started young and had no idea what the prophetic was, I often felt the Lord's heart rise within me and would share it with our congregation because I couldn't contain it.

I remember as a thirteen-year-old being overcome with sadness and tears that were not my own as the Lord spoke to my heart about people who wanted to give up on life. I got up and shared it publicly and many came forward to receive ministry and some salvation. Though many times in the moment I would only feel the nearness and the power of the Lord, later on I would be met by questions and opinions of others that felt painful and I began to question myself and my motives. This became a place in which the fear of man started to speak and eventually lead in my life.

The fear didn't seem as prominent in my younger years, but I do remember the first Sunday I was invited to sing on our worship team as a thirteen-year-old. During our practice, I was so aware of myself (and my lack) that I told my mom, our worship pastor, I couldn't sing for the service. The fear of failure had so gripped me that I just couldn't imagine standing up there in front of everyone, but I also knew I would not be able to worship the Lord being so preoccupied with myself. Maybe this is a lofty thought for a thirteen-year-old, but it was true in my heart that longed to love the Lord well.

Because my exposure was negligible in these seasons, and I was able to move beyond the fear and bring a sacrifice to the Lord. Moving to Redding and attending our ministry school, with far more public presence than my small church in South Africa, further exposed this fear in me. The fear of man operating in my life had a goal—to get me to live small and hidden. It attempts to diminish all potential influence we could have for the Lord's glory and manage the size of our effect on the world around us till it's nil.

I lived in constant tension, wanting to be totally given to the Lord but afraid I would overwhelm the people around me. It was when I got hired on staff here at Bethel that the pressure really started to increase. People can create a wonderful environment for us to thrive in, but there are so many things that a healthy environment, full of the love of God, will uncover in us. Unless we are willing to look at it and lay down our own self-protection and let the Lord do a great work, it will continue to be pressed upon until we surrender it to Him.

So long as the fear of failure existed in me, I would need to protect myself from anyone seeing my weakness—which is impossible. I believe God, in His mercy, allowed me to continue to increase in favor so that I would eventually come to the end of my rope and let go of my self-constructed protection and let Him have all of me. I now know that the enemy is so afraid when we start moving in our God-given call, and that is when he starts shouting louder. The more I would lead and preach, the more I would hear the voice of intimidation taunting me and telling me to back down and quit. There were weeks and sometimes months when I would feel constantly bombarded by the voice of inadequacy. I remember so many times when I would get up to preach or lead worship. I would feel such a powerful faith in the Lord, and as quickly as I experienced that faith, it would be attacked by the voice of the fear of man, and I allowed it to have a place to influence me. I constantly felt like if I was true to the faith I would be far too much, but if I gave in to the fear of man I would not be enough for those I was leading. Thus, I never felt my best was enough for anything or anyone. I felt like I was constantly trying to figure out how to love God and ensure everyone felt good about me and around me.

The fear of man would tell me that good leadership kept everyone happy at all times and that if I tried harder and gave more, it would be possible. I had come to the place where in my lowest moments, I was considering giving up on ministry in the church, the thing I felt like I was created for. I became so burned out physically that I was utterly exhausted every weekend. I had two viruses, mono and shingles, reactivate in my body a few months prior. I had panic attacks that would cause my heart to beat so hard that my shirt would move from it pounding, and I was doing everything I could to try and stay in the fight for my destiny in the Lord.

THE WORD RELEASES GRACE

That night when Michael prophesied over me, I was lying on the floor under the power of God, telling the Lord I needed a miracle. I remembered something I have heard said many times in our school of ministry—that when God releases a prophetic word over your life, He releases His grace for that word to be accomplished. Grace is released not only for us to receive our salvation but also for those saved by Jesus to walk in a manner worthy of the call (see Ephesians 4:1-3). Grace empowers us to fulfill that which God has spoken. Our Father God is not passive. Not only does He speak life over us, but He empowers the words He has spoken by His Spirit.

EXCHANGING MY SHIELD FOR HIM

So while I was lying there thinking about this, I began to talk to the Lord, saying to Him, "God, if this is You, I need a miracle; I need Your grace to be what empowers this word because I have no power here. You alone know that I have fought this battle for my whole Christian walk." As I lay there debating with this word, the Lord began to show me that the fear of man had been a shield that I had used in my life. I realized that I believed that by listening to its voice, I could adjust myself and preempt what people wanted and thus please them. Fear of man was a filter I could use to discern what people were comfortable with and give them what they wanted, and when you give people what they want, they are happy. The problem with this is that everyone wants something different. It makes you like one of those clowns trying to juggle on a unicycle while his friend keeps throwing more and more things on you to add to the act. The cost of the fear of man far outweighs the benefit. Fear robbed my obedience to the Lord and all my courage. It became a slave driver, and no matter how hard I tried I still would not be enough to please everyone.

As He began to reveal this to me, in my thoughts I knew I was at a crossroads and that I had to be willing to let the whole pile of things I was juggling fall. I had already come to the end of my rope, and the reality that I couldn't keep up had already hit me. I began to say, "Lord, I lay down my shield of the fear of man; God, will You be my shield?" I was afraid of what that would mean for me, what would need to change, but I was desperate, and in my heart of hearts I knew that I couldn't live like this anymore. I needed this word to be activated in me more than I needed that protection. There was no way I could keep striving. My body was exhausted, my heart empty and insecure, and I knew deep down that babying my fear was no longer an option; I needed breakthrough.

That night I got off the ground and went back to my seat. I didn't feel like the fear of man had died that instant, but I knew something was different. I could feel I had received something I needed. I had received a seed that if I could pay attention to it and nurture it, something could change.

The next day I woke up and could feel something significant had happened. All I knew to do was begin to declare what I had partnered with the night before: "Lord, I surrender my shield of the fear of man to You, and I ask You to be my shield." This became a daily declaration for me as I began to walk out what I had received.

There have been many times when I have heard stories of people encountering God or receiving words like these, and at that moment everything changed for them. That moment was not the case for me. Nothing external had changed yet, though I knew I had received something. That night in October, I received a word in seed form. God had planted something in my heart, and He was inviting me to partner with Him to see it come into the fullness that He had already made a way for.

After receiving this word (about the fear of man dying) and surrendering to the Lord at that moment, there were so many moments when I still felt very afraid. That fear caused me to want to pick up my shield I had previously used and hide behind it, but something had shifted in my heart; I now knew that that shield was not helpful any longer. I remember standing outside my office in one of these moments, knowing I was entering a tough meeting in which someone was not very happy with me. Usually, I would plan my response and figure out how to move through the meeting with as little pain as possible, but now I was leaning against my doorpost, saying under my breath: "You are my shield and my reward (Genesis 15:1), You are my refuge and You go before me, and when You go before me I will not be shaken (Psalm 16:8). Jesus, teach me what true love is—how do I truly love this person as You do without the need to please them? I give You my shield of fear and ask You to be my shield." I said a version of this prayer most days for months.

What I used to believe would protect me I now realized was a great hindrance to the fullness of what the Lord was drawing me into.

Romans 12:1 talks about being transformed by renewing our minds. Through prophetic words, God will lead us to this new way of operating through prophetic words if we will let Him. When we receive these invitations from the Lord to change the way we think, it requires us to step into a new operating system. At that point, this renewal of my mind was not one moment but a daily faith choice to believe what God had said over what I was experiencing. Full of the Spirit, Michael's words released the grace to lay down something I had been carrying for most of my life.

After yielding that to the Lord, I felt like I had more opportunities to partner with fear. I'm not sure if I was more aware, but to me it felt like the word was being tested. In those moments, I often ended up around my friend and coworker Dave Ward, who would remind me about the word without hesitation. Dave became someone in my life who was willing to tell me the truth and hold me to the word that the Lord had spoken. He carried a yes to Jesus that always inspired me; he had seen the fear of man bow in his life in many ways. It is not always fun for someone to hold you accountable, but I believe it was one of the greatest gifts of my life in that season.

I remember nearly daily declaring, "God, I surrender my shield of the fear of man, and I ask You to be my shield." It was the posture I had to take in order to partner with the word of the Lord and have the truth renew my mind. It was a reminder to my heart and a promise to the Lord that I had laid it down. This process of laying down went on for three months. I began to realize how much of my life had been managed by this lie.

It felt like the Lord was graciously chipping away at this giant boulder standing in my way, one that I had tried to move many times on my own. I truly believe much of the burnout, the panic attacks, the viruses my body was fighting, and the overwhelming exhaustion I was experiencing had been me trying to navigate around this giant boulder in my life. Like the Israelites circling the mountain for 40 years, I was exhausted by trying to move around fear when I just needed to let the Lord kill it and embrace living in the consequences and victory of obedience to His voice.

Throughout my life, particularly in the years preceding this word about the fear of man, I had received many words about being a "voice" or a "mother to the nations." These words were about speaking and teaching, and even some about filling stadiums and declaring the Word of the Lord. Though to some those words might sound exciting, to me they felt like an impossible pressure. I used to weep and wrestle with these words when I would get them, telling the Lord that I didn't want them because I didn't want the pressure from them. I was already full of anxiety and fear from being a pastor in ministry, afraid of four people's opinions of me, let alone four hundred or, worse yet, forty thousand. I saw some of the persecution my leaders met as they stood for what they believed in, and I felt too weak to face even a small percentage of what they did. But God, in His mercy and great faithfulness, saw my heart and desire for Him despite my fear. He saw me offer my meager five loaves and two fish and somehow saw it fit to do a great miracle in me, and what a miracle it was.

THE DAY EVERYTHING CHANGED

On January 14, 2020, on a regular old Tuesday afternoon, the Holy Spirit sovereignly moved in my life in a way that I still tremble when I share it. Even now as I write, deep emotion stirs up inside of me in my gratitude for how God met me that day. The Monday preceding, I was in attendance at our weekly BSSM (Bethel School of Supernatural Ministry) staff meeting, where we talked through the details of the week. My leader, Gabe Valenzuela, told us there had been a schedule change. Our senior leader and one of my heroes, Bill Johnson, was coming into the class that Tuesday to share about revival history and show the various artifacts he had from previous revivals. This day in school was always one of my favorites. Bill would take time to share stories of miracles and healings from previous healing revivals. He would show videos of the Holy Spirit sweeping through rooms and touching people powerfully. We saw crutches from Kathryn Kuhlman's ministry that someone left behind because they were healed, and we heard of the great men and women of God who paid a high price to carry the precious anointing. The faith in the room and the hunger for more were always tangible, something I have always desired.

The problem was that as I checked my calendar for when he was scheduled to come, I noticed that we already had scheduled a "home group leaders training" time for our students in our leadership program. In our second year school program, we divide our students into small groups of about 15, and we appoint student leaders over these groups and empower them to lead their peers. I was in charge of doing two or three formal pieces of training for these 80 student leaders, many who were leading groups for the first time; this was our final session. Weeks before, the schedule had reflected that this was an excellent time to pull them out of class for my assistant third year students and me to do a training session. I immediately decided to cancel the training as being in that class with Bill was far more valuable in the big picture than training with my team and me.

As I thought this, the Lord interrupted my thought and spoke to my spirit not to cancel. I argued in my mind with Him; it felt ridiculous to do training when Bill was teaching on such a vital topic. This time with Bill was an essential time of impartation for all of our students; they needed to be a part of it. Still, I felt the Lord lead me to continue with our training because He said He wanted to move powerfully in our midst. The Lord told my heart that He would move mightily in our training, and it would spill out to the rest of the school from there.

Now, I want to tell you that it may be exciting for some to hear, but for me it sounded ludicrous. How would my little training in a side room, where we were to talk about the logistics of leading people and how to set up an environment for personal growth, be the place where the Holy Spirit would crash in, especially since Bill Johnson was next door talking about revival? Some would have the faith for that, but honestly I could not fathom it. Not only could I not fathom it, but fear began to creep up in my heart. I began to wonder about the message it would send to other leaders and Bill if I chose to continue with my training as planned. I want to add that no one has ever done or said anything to make me think this way here at Bethel. But part of my upbringing in the school system in South Africa had a firm emphasis on honoring leaders, elders, and authority, and it was quite militant. Though unintended, my sensitive heart somehow learned that fear was the best way to stay out of trouble.

MY FEAR OF EMBARRASSING MY LEADERS

What was interesting about this choice that had presented itself was that a couple of days before this moment, I was sitting with a spiritual mom and counselor, sharing the struggle of saying yes to the Lord and the words He had spoken over my life. I was sharing with her about the word I had received and how I was walking out the tension of surrendering my shield of the fear of man to the Lord. While talking with her about this, I discovered the two things that made me most afraid to yield to the Holy Spirit fully. It was the fear of embarrassing my leaders or having them misunderstand my heart. The other fear was people thinking I just wanted attention. Two things God was about to deal with.

Despite my fear, I knew I needed to continue saying yes to what I felt the Lord speaking and prepare to apologize if I got it wrong (something I never wanted to do). I kept my training and explained nothing, not because I was not afraid but because God had to become my shield.

MAKING COVENANT WITH GOD

The next day, Tuesday the 14th, we held the training, which was fine. Nothing spectacular happened, and the whole time I thought I had missed it and was willing to receive any consequence if I had gotten it wrong. But at the end of the training, after my team had wonderfully led our students in the practicals of leadership, I got up to close the session in prayer. As I began to pray what seemed like an ordinary prayer, the fire of the Lord started to hit me, I began to feel incredibly hot, and boldness came over me. I have had moments like this before, but the reaction in the room felt far more powerful. As I prayed, I began to talk about making covenant with God and forsaking all other loves. I started declaring, "We live before one thing—an empty cross and an empty grave."

As I made this declaration, the Holy Spirit began to touch people in the room, and people started to encounter the fire of God. In all honesty, I can't quite tell you the rest of the events in sequence because the room became quite chaotic, but there was no mistaking—God was moving. Some people began to make a covenant verbally, pledging themselves fully to the Lord; some were feeling heat all over their body; others were standing on their chairs shouting "yes" to Jesus, while others were weeping in His presence. People started falling out under the power of God. The room was electric. God was there in a powerful way. I had to cancel my next training session for our third years and have them join us in the room because one thing I have learned from my leaders is that if God is moving in a room, you follow Him and not your agenda (or my comfort).

FOLLOWING THE HOLY SPIRIT

I did my best to follow what I felt the Holy Spirit was saying at that time, knowing He didn't need perfection but simply our attention and desire for Him to move. There came the point where I remembered what the Lord had said—that what He was going to do in that little side room, He wanted to do in the big school meeting room. It was minutes before the end of our main class session, so I asked the students who were able to walk across the hall into the main auditorium because I felt the Lord wanted to release this to the whole class. We quietly snuck into the back of the room, and I inched to the front where my friend Dave was closing the day to release students into a break before their following classes.

When Dave saw me walk up, I asked if I could share something. I got on my knees quietly and felt to say what I had said in the other room when the fire of the Lord began to fall. I said, "God, we live before one thing—an empty cross and an empty tomb." I thought this was the big moment and expected something to happen, but it was just silent as I waited. I remember it feeling like an eternity, and I am not always the most patient in those moments, so I decided I needed to count to thirty in my head, peeking one eye open every ten seconds to see if anything was happening. A few minutes felt like an eternity, but I knew I just needed to try to be obedient. Nothing significant happened, so I returned the mic to Dave, and he closed the day. Our students wanted to take a look at some of the things Bill had brought to the room that day, so as Dave closed the day he gave them the option to hang around for a bit to see them.

Some of our students started stacking the chairs while the other seven hundred started moving around to look at the artifacts and get to where they needed to go next. I remember feeling like maybe I had missed the Lord and a little disappointed that the fire of the Lord we had experienced in the side room had not filled the sanctuary. I did not feel like a failure at that moment; something had already started to change in me over the last three months of laying down my shield. I just didn't know it yet. The message of taking risks in the Lord that had been encouraged and modeled by our leaders in our environment was swirling around my head. I wasn't afraid because I knew that I had done my best to be obedient, which was all He asked of me. God was catalyzing what I had been yielding to, and like a snowball rolling down a hill, the momentum was building and my faith in Jesus was growing.

HIS RAW POWER

As I walked off the stage to pack up my things and leave for the day, the Lord interrupted my thoughts and asked me to begin to lay my hands on people. I thought it was an odd time, but I was in the mode of following, so I did. People were lining up to look at the various pieces of revival history that were around the room like one would do in an art gallery. In my mind, I thought I would go to the back of the room and not make a scene, but instantly a vision flashed before me. I saw myself reaching my hands out as I prayed and touching people on their faces right in the front section. I had a split second to respond as I was already up and moving. Looking at my friend Dave, I said, "This could ruin everything," knowing that if what I was sensing in my spirit would come to fruition, holy chaos just might ensue, and all the order that was currently experienced would be shaken up. There was a holy boldness rising in me, and something in me knew God was about to move powerfully among us.

In a matter of seconds from walking off the stage, I walked toward the first person standing in the line. I leaned forward, with both hands out to touch the face of the person in front of me. As I did, it was like a thousand volts of electricity hit my body and engulfed me from the top of my head to the soles of my feet. The raw power of God hit my head and flowed intensely through my body. I felt it shoot out of my hands and hit the person right as I touched their face. It was one of those moments you simply could not make up, even in the best-case scenario. God was moving in power, doing what only He could do. The person I had leaned forward to touch flew back under the power of the Holy Spirit, and I knew the same power of God that I could feel flowing through me was there to touch those all around me.

I HAD TO YIELD

As this was all happening, I knew I had to yield to the Lord at this moment; it wasn't time to worry about what was happening next or all the things I needed to accomplish before I went home. Something was happening, and it was holy. I had never felt the presence of God like this before. This power of God was so profoundly upon me and moving through me. My leader Bill Johnson often would say that when God encounters you, it is not time to analyze but time to receive and enjoy it. I am not sure the power I felt was physically enjoyable, but the freedom and courage I now had were supernatural and the very thing I had been crying out for. This was a holy moment, and God in His mercy chose to rest on me. At that point, I was willing to do anything He asked not to mess that up. I could sense that I was in a *Kairos* moment, and I was invited to go somewhere deep in the Lord I had never dared to go, and it required me to be fully given to Him; nothing else could compete for my attention at that moment. I truly think I could have chosen my way out of what was to come at that moment. I could have backed out to preserve my dignity, but something too powerful was happening, and I am so grateful for the grace Jesus gave me to stay in the moment with Him.

I remember asking my assistant to message my husband and tell him I wouldn't be coming home right away and to let him know what was happening, though I was not even entirely sure what was happening. From that moment on, everything becomes blurred.

THE MIND OF GOD

As I made room, the holy presence of God started powerfully coursing through my body, and as I yielded in my heart to what the Lord was doing it was like my mind's cognitive thoughts became blank. As my thoughts became silent, suddenly it was like I was hearing God as clearly as my own thoughts had been before that. There was one thought, one focus, what He was saying, and honestly it was all I could think. I began to sense the anointing (His presence) and see Him rest on people. It was purposeful; the Holy Spirit had an agenda. I had never ministered like this before. I wasn't moving from person to person as they directed me but was being wholly directed by the Lord. I would watch the Holy Spirit rest on some; I could perceive it and see it. At times it was with my physical eyes and other times a perception, but it was as powerful and clear as me stating a fact about my life. In the spirit, it looked like God shone a light on those people; His presence's tangible peace and warmth drew me toward them. The power of the Spirit had awakened the eyes of my heart, and He was allowing me to experience some of His world in a very real way.

The Holy Spirit was directing me with His resting, showing me whom He was highlighting, and making way for an ignition point to catalyze the hearts of His people. As I laid hands on these people whom the Spirit highlighted, they would powerfully encounter the Lord. Many would shake violently, fall over, or weep deeply as He moved. I remember laying my hand on a spiritual daughter of mine; I could feel the freedom of the Lord upon her, and she began to roar loudly. She was usually relatively quiet and has a very sweet and tender demeanor, but the Lord was breaking off silence and releasing His boldness into her this day. The thoughts of God were so beautiful and liberating, not critical or harsh.

As I moved with the Holy Spirit, I began to feel deep emotion start washing over me. The nearness and tenderness of God began to undo me from the inside out. As I ministered, I started to weep uncontrollably as I felt His longing for His people and their freedom. At this moment in particular, I was able to discern people's pain or disappointment, too, but I never felt angst or frustration from the Lord. I would feel His kindness and compassion as He invited me to pray for His love to permeate deeply into their hearts. Though He was so tender, there were other times when I felt His intensity toward the enemy's assault and His possessive love that roars over our thoughts and beliefs. God began to show me the power and sweetness of His love, and He didn't apologize for the tension of the two. The purity of God's love was so convicting, and whether intense or sweet it was directed to bring freedom and wholeness to His children.

THE RESTING PLACE OF GOD

I am sure you can imagine this was not clean nor dignified. The pure power flowing through my little frame was more than my body could bear. This kind of encounter required the surrender of everything—my fear, my dignity, my mind, my body; it required it all and more. I shook violently as waves of intense heat and surges of holy power apprehended my entire being. It was like God had put me on like a glove and was directing every moment. For hours I moved around the room, yielding to the Spirit's leading and laying hands on people by grasping their faces in the palms of my hands. Words started to flow from my mouth as I approached some standing in the room: "God, thank You for this resting place, this prepared place," came from His heart to them as I wept under the anointing of the Holy Spirit.

God was teaching me my first lesson at this moment. As I was saying this phrase and approaching different people, the heart of the Father was being revealed to me—He is looking for a resting place.

As I declared this, many people would begin to weep and cripple over as the weight of His glory would overshadow them, and others would shake violently under His power. Oftentimes it was as I would approach them, before I could even touch them. His words were weighty and transformative, doing the work in their hearts. The overwhelming presence of the one true living God was there in greater measure, and He was doing what He has always longed for. He was communing with His people.

I was completely and utterly undone. All I could do was simply cooperate with the Holy Spirit's agenda and follow His timing on what to say and when to lay hands, and He did the rest. I had never experienced anything like this before or heard of it. Even as I write this again, I have tears streaming down my face as I feel God rest on me, reminding us of His goodness and faithfulness. This is what Jesus paid for—for His Bride to know Him, to know the power of His mighty Spirit, and walk in full connection with Him.

HE CONTINUED THE WORK HE STARTED

After nearly three hours of laying hands on people, I began to "come around," if you could say that. I had lost all track of time and began to realize two of the pastors in our school and brothers in Christ had been carrying me around the room as my body had not been able to stand under the power of God flowing through it. I was stumbling all over, just trying to stay upright, and I had sweat through all of my clothes because of His fire resting on me. My eyes were nearly swollen shut from weeping so profoundly and for so long. I was undone by Him, and I had never felt so free. That evening the only option I had was to be driven home, and as I wept in the passenger seat, in my mind I asked the Lord if He would help me be a mom to my two small children because, at that moment, I could hardly move under the weight of the glory of God.

Stumbling into my home, I fell to my knees at the threshold of our door, weeping in the presence of our holy King. My son, who was four years old, approached me to ask what was wrong. As we embraced at the front of my home, I explained to him that I was crying what we call "happy tears" and that God was touching me with His love, which was a good thing. He instantly understood, and a smile came to his face. My husband helped me from the ground, and within 30 minutes of being home, the Lord gave me grace as I had asked, and I was able to make a simple dinner and get my kids to bed. I never fully felt His power lift from me, but a fresh grace came on me to love my family well. After getting my children to bed, some of my spiritual children from South Africa were visiting Bethel and had been in the room that day and came to our home to visit us. They had watched the display of God that day and had received powerfully from the Holy Spirit. They had spent three years here in Redding, under my pastoral leadership, and had returned for a visit, but none of us anticipated that this was what God would do. I sat on my couch with them and my husband, and they were, of course, curious to know what had happened that afternoon. As I started to share with them, the power of the Holy Spirit hit me again in the same way it had earlier that day, and I began to weep uncontrollably as I felt Him rest on me. I began to cry and shake as I shared, unable to communicate effectively, nor could I fully comprehend what had happened. This weeping and shaking went on until I went to sleep that night.

WEEPING ON THE HIGHWAY

The following day, I had to wake up early for a preachers' meeting. This meeting started at 7:30 a.m., which is no time for a meeting. I had slept hard that night and woke up feeling groggy, likely because my body had withstood what one would explain as a freight train going through it the day before. I got up quickly as I woke up late, threw on some jeans and a T-shirt, and grabbed my makeup, thinking that I would do it on my way to work. My home is very close to our local highway, and about a minute into driving I hit the on ramp. As I merged with the traffic, seemingly out of nowhere, the Holy Spirit fell on me in my car. I began to weep uncontrollably as I was driving to work. I had no understanding of what I was weeping about, but I knew that the presence of God was doing a work far too deep for me to comprehend.

When I arrived at Bethel, I could hardly walk to my meeting. It took me 20 minutes to get from my car to the upper room where the meeting was held. I was having to crawl down the hall, and you could imagine the struggle to make it up the stairs. I was met with many alarmed staff members' faces as I entered the room. I'm sure they thought something awful had happened with how hard I cried. I reassured them that this was simply the Lord, and it was good. That day we were working on creative communication and sharing some writing we had done, but all I could think about was how beautiful Jesus was.

This was the moment that I realized this mighty work the Lord was doing in me was the beginning of the breaking of the fear of man in my life. Previously, I would have felt afraid of missing the assignment and pressure to pull myself together and exceed the expectations of my leaders, but now I felt no fear and yet absolute honor. Everything we were doing in our meeting was beautiful; it was powerful, and I could participate with my whole heart but not have to shift into performance to hit the target. The sweetness of the Lord was overshadowing me and the grace to give Him my yes was there. All of the fear about how others perceived me no longer had power because His power was now available to me.

As people shared their writing, I was so moved by each of their gifts, not feeling insecure or like I had to strive. Then my turn came, and I shared a very non-profound, very childlike poem about Jesus, and though it may not have moved anyone in the room, I could tell it moved His heart. Before, I would have wanted everyone to approve of what I had said, but now I just wanted to be a blessing. I was being recalibrated to the voice and opinion that matters most, the voice of my Lord. I had done nothing to deserve this, but His mercy was more than sufficient for me; His mercy had hunted me down and pursued me, met me in my insufficiency, and now I was being set free.

I used to think that if I didn't live with a measure of the fear of man, I would not love people well, but the fact is that I was loving them better. I did not lose the honor for my leaders when the fear of the Lord encountered me; my honor for them remained. It was just pure now and was seeking to serve. Not looking for my leaders' or anyone else's approval moved me from needing to be served with their thoughts about me to being able to bring a pure offering, seeking to serve the room and not be served myself. Their affirmation is still a wonderful and powerful thing. It just wasn't my source for survival any longer.

CHAPTER 2

THE PURPOSE OF
THE ENCOUNTER

This wild and holy encounter did not stop at day one; it continued for nearly six weeks. The Lord was fulfilling the word spoken over me in 2019. He met me in my surrender and gave Himself to me as the gift. Every day for six weeks, I experienced a mighty outpouring of His Holy Spirit upon me as an individual, and I watched as He touched people's lives through an earthen vessel. We can often attribute these moments to people we think are unique or special and thus disqualify ourselves from a touch from God, but I believe these moments only happen by His mercy.

THE WEIGHT OF HIS PRESENCE

For six weeks the Holy Spirit took a hold of all that was shakable to leave that which is eternal. After my preachers' meeting, I stumbled into my office, where I was supposed to have meetings all day. The problem was I could no longer do what I had always done; even if I tried, I couldn't because the weight of glory resting on me was changing everything. I remember lying on my office floor hugging a fuzzy white pillow and weeping for hours into this pillow as I played a song by Upper Room over and over again called "Open the Scroll." In fact, I would encourage you to put it on while you read this chapter and let the Holy Spirit minister to you through this powerful declaration.

This song repeats the word *holy* at least twenty times, I would assume. As I lay on my office floor weeping, waves of His glory and holiness would wash over me. In the beauty of His majesty, the words "open the scroll and break the seal" repeating over and over, my spirit began to resonate with this powerful truth—there is only one worthy to break open the mysteries and blueprints of Heaven over our lives, that is Jesus Himself. God was awakening my being to the power and worthiness of the Lamb that was slain. He was worthy to break open every limitation in my life, and He was present at this moment and giving Himself to me without hesitation and with no limits. He was not just Emmanuel in the Christmas story, but He is Emmanuel now, today. Every aspect of Him was present, everything that I needed, everything that I had been crying out for was available to me because He was there. It was too much to bear at times, and the realization of the incredible availability of God to us was too wonderful and so provoking and convicting.

HE DID NOT LIFT

This continued day in and day out; this intense and powerful presence of God resting upon me and moving within me did not lift and did not cease. I couldn't manufacture it, I couldn't make it happen, I simply had to yield when His Spirit would come upon me. Sometimes it was at church, which was more ideal than when it occurred in the grocery store. Despite the embarrassment that one would expect to feel, I seldom even took a moment to think about it. It was like the power and beauty of God I was experiencing took all my attention and I simply had nowhere else to look and nothing else I wanted to entertain. It was so holy and magnificent I did not even consider quenching it for the sake of appearance. What God was doing in me was like finding a long-lost treasure, and all of a sudden the surroundings just did not matter.

During these six weeks, I could not talk most of the time. I remember being in meetings and my leaders asking me what was happening to me. When I would open my mouth to try and share deep and breathless sobs would come from my innermost being. The weight of the glory of the Lord would fall upon me and I would slide down from my chair onto the floor as His holiness would engulf every part of my body.

Nobody knew that the Lord was breaking off the fear of man in my life because I could not talk about it. Every time I went to explain I would simply sob and wail in the presence of the Lord. I did, however, have many people walk up to me and let me know in this time of encounter as I would lay hands on them that insecurity and the fear of man would leave them immediately.

WHY OUR ENCOUNTERS MATTER

I've heard it said before, and it is true now more than ever: "You teach what you know, but you impart what you live."

People often ask why we need an encounter and why we need God to touch our lives. In fact, I was one of those people. I have loved God all my life, and I got saved when I was three years old listening to Psalty the Singing Songbook. Psalty was crying and saying: "You can sing and sing until you are blue in the face, but if it is not from your heart, it's not praise." I was so bothered by Psalty's sadness; it felt to my three-year-old heart that God was sad when we just sang songs and didn't mean it. At that moment, moved by the sadness in God's heart, I gave my heart to Jesus. I think deep down, I was responding with a desire to live an authentic Christian life, one that said yes to singing (living) authentically from my heart toward Jesus and meaning every word. I now know it was the wooing of the Holy Spirit drawing me into my destiny in Jesus to be one who would love Him fully and be completely devoted to Him.

I followed Jesus through my childhood and my teen years into young adulthood. But I didn't know He wanted to be so close to me that I couldn't tell between Him and me. I knew Jesus loved me, but the thought of Him being that close to me felt vulnerable, too vulnerable for such a perfect and powerful God. I saw God like a coach in the sky with a big clipboard, telling me the plays and yelling corrections as I tried to figure out how to do what was in His heart. I felt like I was supposed to please Him, behaving so that I could be His daughter instead of living from the place of security as His daughter. True sons and daughters don't question their value, and we have nothing to prove; they live from their value, and their actions carry and display it everywhere they go. I didn't know that value yet because I hadn't fully grasped the powerful revelation that He had given His Holy Spirit to live in me, lead me, and empower me.

I had often heard encounters spoken of, but I did not have a high value for them. They felt too intangible, so I could not grasp their true power and our need for them. I thought they were happenstance, something that could or could not happen to you, which felt risky and unfair. There were other times I would hear people sharing about an encounter and I received it as "something that happened" to this person that was heavenly and amazing, but I could not grasp how deeply personal it was for God, not just for them. To think of the almighty God longing to be personally connected and living powerfully in me was hard to grasp. It was common for me to think of the Holy Spirit as a "thing." It was more accessible for me to think of Him as the glory, fire, rain, or a presence, but that is profoundly impersonal and not what a true encounter with God is. Relegating the Spirit to a "thing" left me powerless in this equation. I had missed that not only was I impacted by God's love for me, but God was impacted by my longing for Him. My encounter woke me up to the reality that I was not encountering a thing or a presence; I was encountering the living God through the power of His very own Spirit. The person of my encounter was the person of the Holy Spirit, the Spirit of God. All these people were experiencing great freedom because of the person of the Holy Spirit living and active inside of me. Yielding to Him had made the room He was asking for to move freely without the restraint of my fear. He was now touching people in the same way that He was touching me. The Holy Spirit wouldn't simply let this be a moment for one person, but He was looking for a people.

The God of all creation, the King of Glory, is looking for a people to dwell with. This is not new news; this has been going on since the beginning of the creation of man. Our God is a God of union and communion, a God of connection who wants to live fully and wholly connected to His people in such a powerful way that we would be one with Him and unified as His body. This powerful union can only happen by the indwelling and residing of the Holy Spirit.

This was the prayer of Jesus in John 17 for His disciples, and for all disciples to come—that we would be one with the Father as He is one with the Father. This is the dream that is on the heart of God for all of His people—that there would be no separation between Him and His body—and He will not rest until we step into this fullness, nor will the church.

Presence matters. In this technological day and age, we can text, call, FaceTime, or Zoom, but nothing replaces that moment when you are reunited with the person you love. I live halfway around the world from my family; the Lord has called us here to Redding, but we deeply love many back home in South Africa. While I am incredibly grateful for modern-day technology and the way that we can connect through it, I eagerly wait for the day when I fly into the airport and meet my loved ones face to face. Presence matters. God knows this because He designed us to live in His presence, walking with Him daily. God is the God of love, His nature is love, and therefore His nature is one that longs for connection and to be known by those whom He loves and those who love Him.

WHAT ARE ENCOUNTERS?

An encounter is a meeting with God, and when we meet with God, we are changed. Encounters are not limited to outward manifestations and violent shaking, as I had. They can look like many things: a whisper, a moment of healing, the presence of His peace where anxiety once was. Though they are not necessarily violent or loud, we should also not limit encounters with the living God to what we prefer or can comprehend. Too often we jump to conclusions about what God is or is not doing, but we often need time to let Him do a deep work and let the fruit speak for itself.

I could not comprehend what God was doing in me in those days of radical encounter. I could not fathom the magnitude of what He was doing in my life. I have spent nearly the last three years unpacking and stewarding what I received in that time, and I am sure I will continue to for the rest of my life. In this one moment, this one touch from the precious Holy Spirit, my whole life was instantly changed. I am a different person. I am free, I am freer than I have ever been, and I was freed from years of struggle by one touch of His hand. But walking out that freedom and carrying it in a way that gives God glory and honor will require intentionality on my part. My encounter with God catalyzed a process already working in me. He accomplished in me in that short time what decades of hard work could never achieve. He showed me in those six weeks what a life fully surrendered to Him could be and feel like. He allowed me to taste freedom and fullness I had only heard stories of, but that encounter was an invitation to more. It was a taste of a Kingdom that He was inviting me to carry within me to bring His prayer to life: "on earth as it is in Heaven."

Encountering God goes beyond the moment we feel Him near or moving; it goes far beyond a good testimony. These moments of power, passion, or freedom in the Holy Spirit are invitations to know Him more, to seek and find. The tension lies in receiving the outpouring, not analyzing it too soon, and learning to steward it in due season.

I feel cautious as I write this because I have seen either side over-emphasized, and neither way produces the fruit we are truly looking for. Some criticize the encounter because they have seen so many have encounters and not change or steward the change God deposited. In contrast, others criticize the stewardship of encounters as a restrictive "form." I could not emphasize either over the other but invite you to walk with one in each hand, being willing to carry the tension of it in your relationship with the Lord.

The shaking and power of the God I experienced were vital to my deliverance and transformation. God knew I needed it, and He willingly gave it to me. I know that I needed every ounce of the outpouring and awakening of the Holy Spirit to walk in what I am walking in now, and interrupting it would have been devastating. I could not touch it with strategy; it would have felt like taking a tool to His altar; it was holy and Jesus had to have His way to accomplish what I needed. I had to not only surrender to the power of His personhood but I had to yield to His timing and way. For months after this, I had no idea what God had done in me, but through discipline in my time with Jesus, the Holy Spirit taught me of all He had done and is still teaching me to this day.

When we have profound moments with the Lord, yielding to them and allowing Him to do a great work in us is vital. When the Holy Spirit is tangibly upon you, it is not time to be introspective but time to receive. It's the season after that we must take the time to press into His work in us and pursue His heart to know His intention. This is a covenant, not just a moment, and while moments of encounter are vital and valuable in covenant, it is the day-to-day pursuit that anchors them and causes them to flourish. If we let the seed He deposits take root in our lives and nurture it until it grows into maturity, we will bear the fruit of the word. Receiving the seed is just the first step. We must nurture it so that the world can reach out to taste and see His goodness from our lives lived in full connection with Him.

To think that this violent shaking for six weeks was the extent of His availability would be ludicrous. There is so much more in Him, and there is so much more about Him. There is so much more that He has for me and you that if we were to ask for it now, I believe He would respond to us as He did to His disciples in John 16:12 (NASB), saying, *"I have many more things to say to you, but you cannot bear them at the present time."* An encounter with God is an invitation to more in Him and a lifelong relationship of pursuing and being pursued by the King of all. As we seek real relationship with the Lord, we create space for the more of Him we desire.

THE NEED FOR THE HOLY SPIRIT

The passage in John 16 I just referred to became so profound to me (and I will write about it more in chapters to come) because it holds the promise of the Holy Spirit. Starting in John 14, Jesus comforts His disciples as He prepares them for His death and shares with them that He will no longer be with them. He makes them the promise that He will send another (just like Him) who will be with them always. This promise of His Spirit is a massive turning point for every believer because it is God dwelling within us, empowering us with Himself, always. I became so blatantly aware of this in the six weeks of my life-changing encounter with the Lord Himself. **The Holy Spirit is absolutely vital in the Christian life.**

When I say vital, I mean absolutely paramount in every way. If I could shout it from the rooftops like a rooster every morning or set up a billboard in every church and highway, I would.

One of the deepest grievances of my heart in my encounter with the Lord was that I realized that though I had not done it intentionally, I had been willing to try this Christian life in my own strength when He was always available to me. I grieved the Spirit's heart by failing to recognize His availability and my need for Him. Why would I want to do life without the very presence of God with me? I needed this holy shaking that I experienced to awaken me to the mighty power of the Spirit of God who does not just live in the heavens but is available to every believer in Jesus Christ and how much I truly needed Him.

WAITING FOR HIS LEADING

During these six weeks, God started moving so profoundly in our environment that it was hard to know where it began and ended. We started to have evening meetings in which hundreds of people would gather almost nightly just to worship Jesus and host His presence. The people in our congregation and our school so honor when God touches people that they come humbly to receive prayer whenever possible. Often at the beginning of a meeting, right before worship would start, hungry and humble believers would come up to me and ask for me to lay hands on them. In years past, I would have felt pressure to pray right then and there. However, during this time of encounter, I would feel a little nudge from the Holy Spirit encouraging me to first engage our hearts in worship of the King before I ministered. It wasn't that I needed a reminder that this power flowing through me was not me, because it was too obvious for me to forget, but I believe it was to teach me the priority of exalting Him, and from there everything takes its rightful place. I remember politely honoring their hunger but asking people if they wouldn't mind returning for prayer at the end of the service. I had become aware that I could pray for them then and give them what I had freely received, but if we could host the presence of God and welcome Him first, He would come in a way that simply would eclipse everything we had to offer and would exceed all our expectations. I believe this is what the revivalists of old had grasped; they walked in an understanding of the dependence on God that allowed for His true life-altering power to flow. Hosting the Lord and exalting His name creates an atmosphere of welcome and dependence that enables us to see and know His ways.

HE IS LOOKING FOR A RESTING PLACE

Our King longs to be hosted by His people; the precious Holy Spirit longs to be wanted, to be invited, and to be cooperated with. It is the place where we offer all of who we are to Him so that He comes to rest on us markedly.

We all have incredible gifts operating in our lives. These are gifts given by God, and Romans 11:29 says that these gifts are irrevocable. That means these gifts can never be taken away, regardless of how we use them. For example, say I bought my husband a brand-new, top-of-the-line guitar, but the gift was contingent on him playing it five times a week in the evening and practicing specific songs I had chosen. Though my instructions may be beneficial and help him steward well what he had been given, it would not be a gift at all because gifts don't come with conditions. Gifts are freely given, and the receiver can choose what they want to do with what they are given. Now, if my husband never played the guitar or, worse, used it in a damaging way, I may never give my husband a lavish gift like that again, but the guitar is his to use as he sees fit.

In the same way, God has given us gifts and taught us many excellent principles in the desire that we would steward them in our relationship with Him, but He does not and will not control that because He is love, and love always gives a choice. We must not mistake gifts for rewards. So many times we will think the gift on our life is the evidence of the presence of God operating in our lives, but it is actually the fruit of our lives that marks whether we are walking with Him or in our own strength.

In all our options in this world, the Lord invites us to surrender and submit to His Spirit. It is in this place that our gifts no longer operate in our strength but they now operate filled with

His limitless power, and impossibilities begin to bow. Our gifts were meant to be used in cooperation with the power of the Spirit, just as Jesus cooperated with Him while here on earth. It is like the difference between battery power and plugging into an electrical box. Our gifts on their own have some strength but also have many limitations. When we operate in the things of God without dependence on the Holy Spirit, we operate in the limited revelation of what we know of Him, and eventually the power runs out. But when we create a resting place for Him by living in dependence on Him and offering all of ourselves to Him, we become conduits for the power of the Spirit to flow through, fulfilling His desires and bringing Heaven to earth.

This invitation of actual dependence is what I came to know in this encounter. I had received so much training and tools— all are true, sound, and necessary—but they were never meant to operate independently of dependence on God's presence. I needed a baptism in the Holy Spirit and fire to understand that all of the training I had received was not to prove my identity but existed as an invitation to walk in His ways with Him. My gifts and knowledge needed to be constantly filled with His power so that the world could see a demonstration of His glory. I was well on my way to living an independent, principled life of form with no actual power. I truly thought I was pleasing God by doing things for Him, and I had not realized that He wanted to do everything with me, filling every void and strength with Himself.

This yielding to His power is the same reason the disciples had to wait in the upper room. They could only fulfill the commission Jesus had given them once they had received the baptism of the Holy Spirit and His power in order to be obedient to the call. The same goes for us. The call of the Christian life is one of significant risk and reward, but neither can be entered into without our complete dependence on the Lord. Jesus wants to fill us and empower us to do the impossible in our everyday life, but it requires full awareness that we depend on His Spirit.

DO NOT RESIST HIM

As we would worship the Lord during those evening meetings, our praise and welcome would begin to host His presence. Like Ezekiel's river in Ezekiel 47, the tangible presence of God that we could sense in the room before we started worshiping began to rise like that river. It went from ankle-deep, to knee-deep, to waist-deep, until we were fully submerged in this mighty rushing Holy Spirit river that He longed to pour out on His people. When the river of His presence rises, we are welcomed to get swept away in His ways into a Kingdom full of righteous peace and joy, a Kingdom in which nothing is impossible. Even now, as I write, I ache with a longing for a move of the River of God in such a way that we as a people would be swept up and could only go where He was sending us.

There is a deep groan in the spirit, in creation, and in the heart of His people for a manifestation of the glory of God. There is a longing in every created person for a connection so powerful and union so bonded with our Creator that they would live a life far beyond their capabilities. This is our inheritance in Jesus. The life surrendered to the Lord and thus full of His Spirit is a life that carries the promise to know His glory and walk in it (see Ephesians 1:18-23).

When I would pause the personal prayer at the start of the service and ask the people to return later, it would allow each of us to host the Lord by giving Him our attention and love in our worship, setting Him as the priority. As we did this, He would move and stir hunger in His people for more of Him. The people came for prayer after the service, and because we had waited on Him and made room for Jesus to take first place, the Holy Spirit would move so powerfully. The voice of limit and lack that had plagued me for so long had now been replaced with the voice of the Lord. The Holy Spirit whispered to me as I would lay hands on each person that they are His resting place, His prepared place, and that He was longing to pour out His glory upon us.

I would feel led to say this out loud: "God, I honor this resting place, this prepared place, this house to hold Your glory." As I would, before I even touched anyone, people would be touched powerfully by Him. It was not just a few people, but hundreds of us were encountering a God so personal that He would fill us with Himself and call us His home. I remember one meeting that I went to—it was a women's night at our church, and if I'm honest, I was a little nervous for the ladies. They were not our school of ministry students, and I wasn't quite sure how ready they were for the kind of "Hayley" they were going to receive.

The old Hayley would have tried to tone herself down and pull herself together, but she was gone—she had been laid down in a grave and had been resurrected by the mighty power of the Holy Spirit. There was no more scrambling over my notes or anxiety over being too much and offensive; instead, I was still inside. Where before I had hoped to find confidence in myself, I now found it in the fact that God was enough and He was with me. I used to spend so much time apologizing for myself, but I now realized God was moving unapologetically within me, and He was pleased to do so.

I was too far gone in this journey to resist anything God wanted to do, and the thought of resisting God was too painful to consider. In the light of His face, the fears that used to hold me back, the fear of being rejected and cast aside, now bowed to the fact that I only wanted one thing—God. God had become enough for me. No job, no position, no friendships, and no approval of man could ever outweigh what I had experienced in the Lord at this time. This was not something that I thought of or conjured up in my own strength but simply through the power of the holiness of God. In light of the fear of the Lord, the fear of man now felt inconsequential. The lying ploy of the enemy that had robbed from me for 29 years had been broken over the knee of a loving Father who was pursuing me. He had paid a price far too expensive for me to afford and had now placed His Spirit upon me in such a way that I could not bear to refuse Him.

The Lord was moving in me in a way that was so powerful to me, but I am sure to others it was confusing or at least unusual. I had to overcome the worry that some would not understand and that some would but would not be ready to receive it for themselves. I have come to realize that there are times in our journey with the Lord when we have to choose to surrender ourselves to what looks or feels unusual because we sense God is doing a work. There can be a temptation to shut it down or move away because it's too far out of our comfort zone. I must admit that there have been many times when I have had to wrestle through to receive from someone who didn't come packaged as I was comfortable with. We have all wrestled with this at some point, and we have all failed. But the beauty of this is that our own ability qualifies none of us; we are qualified by what Jesus did on the cross for us, and He is looking for a humble heart that is willing to make room for His Spirit to rest on them and He will do that work in us. This night ministering to our women was another moment that required me to step over the line of comfort and give myself to Him without resistance, and when I did He filled me with grace that enabled me to surrender further.

We must not resist God. I can remember times when I rejected what God was doing because I was offended by how it was packaged. I distinctly remember not attending a meeting of a well-known and anointed minister because I was bothered by the criticisms I had heard from others. Other times I would carry judgment in my heart because of how distracting certain manifestations were and wouldn't want to be a part of things I thought were "too much." Of course, not all manifestations or ministers are anointed, but my heart was one of judgment and not hunger.

THE PURPOSE OF THE ENCOUNTER

"Hunger is the evidence of humility."

—Bill Johnson

On this night, ministering to the women, I surrendered myself fully to Jesus once again. The Holy Spirit started moving tangibly, and I began to shake and cry under His presence once again.

God doesn't always come in the way we expect Him to. There are times God will package Himself in a way that we have to surrender our preconceived notions about what it should look like to receive what He has. We are not the ones in charge—He is. When I look at the magnitude of who God is, I realize how small I am, and I am able to hunger for Him. Think about Jesus being birthed in an obscure stable or the people whom God used in the Bible. God doesn't fit our mold; we fit into His.

HE MAKES US HUNGRY FOR HIM

That night I was graciously received by hundreds of women who filled our church sanctuary and listened as I tried to speak through weeping and shaking, yielding to what the Holy Spirit was doing in me. I want you to imagine what it would be like to try and listen to someone speak through weeping, shaking, completely overcome by the power of God. These are the moments that are hard to comprehend. We are all hungry for the Lord, and sometimes these sound like marvelous experiences, but they are also costly.

As those beautiful women sat in the sanctuary that night, God broke all my boxes and began to move. One by one, women made their way forward and filled the altar to receive a touch from the Holy Spirit. I remember my mother was visiting us during this mighty outpouring. That night she was touched powerfully by the Spirit and ministered alongside me to many women.

We invited mothers to fetch their children from childcare as the evening was drawing to a close, but the Holy Spirit was still moving. Seeing mothers bring their small children into the room to encounter God together probably was and is still one of my favorite memories as I am a mother myself. At the end of the night as we were wrapping up, I began to move off of the stage trying to figure out how I would get home as I was under the power of the weight of God. A line began to form beside me of women wanting prayer for more of the Lord.

As I began to pray for women, the line got longer and longer. The women I was nervous about ministering to were so hungry and willing to receive because they wanted Him. Their humility to receive from one of their peers and their ability to see the Holy Spirit moving over potential offense was humbling for me, to say the least. I began moving down the line and praying for woman after woman. Some of our school of ministry ladies had come to support me during this time and they became my catchers. Woman after woman, old and young, began to get touched by the power of the Holy Spirit. I remember looking at the clock before we started praying; it was nearly 11 p.m. and the line of women waiting for prayer started at the front of our sanctuary and wrapped all the way around the room to the exit. Over a hundred women waited for prayer, and He gave Himself without hesitation. The Holy Spirit swept through the room to encounter us all. This demonstration of hunger started to happen all over our environment, and in all of our meetings God was moving markedly in His people.

LOCKDOWN

Early in March, weeks after that first day when this all began, we as a leadership team felt led to do a special event and gathered all the students in our school of ministry together for an all-night worship and prayer event. We had felt to do this because of what God was doing in our environment and we wanted to respond. I'm not sure there is anything more glorious than swarms of God's people gathering together to do one thing: host His presence and experience Him move amongst us.

What was to come I don't think any of us imagined. Amid a mighty outpouring of the Holy Spirit, what we thought was the beginning of a move of God to go to the nations, the nations went into lockdown because of a virus. The day after our all-night prayer and worship event, we had to explain to our students that we had to shut down our school for the unforeseeable future and move to an online platform because there was a virus threatening the world. Covid-19 had been discovered, and the governor of our state had called us all into a hard lockdown in which we weren't allowed to mix with anyone outside of our families in our homes. Amid this mighty outpouring, the enemy had a ploy to grip the world with fear. None of us knew how this virus would pan out, but I don't think any of us could imagine how it was about to affect the whole world.

CHAPTER 3

AWAKE IN AN AWAKENING

HIS VOICE BRINGS CLARITY IN CHAOS

After six weeks of this most powerful and wonderful experience with the person of the Holy Spirit, the world went into complete shutdown. I don't think any of us imagined that what started out as two weeks to slow the spread would become two years of complete and utter confusion throughout the world. The Covid-19 pandemic had begun, and due to all of the unknowns about this virus, *the nations went into complete lockdown.*

I remember lying on my office floor in my home during this time of complete shutdown when we weren't allowed to leave our homes, visit our friends or relatives, let alone do any activities outside all of that, and asking God what was happening. For the last six weeks, I had experienced the most profound encounter of my life and had seen the Lord moving. I was devastated to think that this wave would stop. The two weeks to slow the spread had become six weeks, and we were beginning to see that the six weeks were not going to be enough. The world was in a panic, people losing their loved ones, in fear for their own lives, and for the first time in the history of this generation, we were completely controlled by something outside of our ability.

As I began to seek the Lord there on my office floor, I felt the nearness of the Holy Spirit and I began to weep, this time in deep grief because I was afraid that what God had begun was about to be squashed under the weight of the pressure the world was facing. My encounter had been so life changing, it was like I had been reintroduced to God in a way that I knew in my mind He could exist, but I could never have imagined that it could be real for me. I had met the answer to all of life's problems; I had met a power that no ruler or authority could overcome. I have longed to see revival since a young age, and I had encountered the one who is revival, and I was so afraid that I was going to miss this moment that God had led me to. I was carrying a mandate, a promise, but there was no way to gather the church or anyone, for that matter, and I felt powerless and stuck.

I was walking with a fresh revelation that the precious Spirit of God was available to each and every single one of us, right here right now, and without limitation. I was burning with a holy flame, but I had no place to share or give it away, and I was afraid that it was about to be snuffed out. As I lay there on the floor crying out to the Lord with all my questions and fears, He met me and spoke to me. He didn't answer my questions but said something incredibly simple and yet, in my spirit, it was deeply profound. He said to me, "Hayley, make sure you are awake in an Awakening." I knew in that moment that God was shifting me from the export of what He was doing in me and telling me to just take care of my own heart to steward what I had been given. He was showing me that this was more about building me than building the church or others. I needed time hidden in Him to learn and discover the depth and power of what I had actually received. Like a mother carrying a baby in those first weeks, the Lord was inviting me to become aware that I was carrying His promise, and He wanted all of my attention so that I could protect and nurture it to grow and birth something from His heart.

OUR ATTENTION AND THE SEED SOWN

This was all I needed to hear. God was doing something, He had not stopped, and His hand was in it even though it felt different from what I had anticipated. I think He was speaking directly to what we all face, and not just in the pandemic but what we face in the midst of our glorious encounters with the Lord—distraction. When God works in us, the enemy wants to pull our attention and faith from what God is doing to what he is doing to weaken our resolve. Our attention is one of the greatest commodities being traded in the world today. The spirit realm thrives on attention. Where we give our attention is where we give our focus and our faith. In the natural, the marketing world knows that whatever can get our attention will affect our perception and thus what we focus on and desire.

The words God speaks, written and prophetic, are like powerful revival seeds that are being sown into our lives. When our hearts are hungry and yielded, those seeds are able to take root in the soil of our heart and have the potential to grow and flourish to become more than just fruit but a tree that bears much fruit. When Michael Koulianos prophesied over me three months before I had the tangible touch from the Lord, his words were carrying the DNA of Kingdom transformation empowered by the Spirit of God. They were seed sown in my heart. His word was one of Kingdom origin (not mere man), a declaration that was formed in the mind of God; Jesus desired that the fear of man was going to die in my life. When I gave my attention and surrendered to the word of the Lord and took off the mocking lie of the enemy, the seed of truth began to outgrow the weed of fear in my heart. The enemy knows that he cannot compete with the authority and power of God, but he can compete for our attention and affection, which determines how we steward the truth in our hearts. We as image bearers of the Lord have been given all authority in the name of Jesus (see Matthew 28:18), but we must walk in His ways to wield it. When we grasp the powerful truth of what that means, we become unstoppable to the enemy. When I surrendered to the ways of the Spirit of God in that moment, I welcomed His empowering presence to come in and reveal to me a way of life lived hidden in Jesus rather than in the lies of the world.

In Matthew 13:1-23 Jesus tells a parable about a sower who sows seed. He unveils the power of competition for our attention and affection but also just how powerful and fruitful our lives can be when we tend to the soil of our hearts.

> *And He told them many things in parables, saying, "Behold, the sower went out to sow; and as he sowed, some seeds fell beside the road, and the birds came and ate them up. Others fell on the rocky places, where they did not have much soil; and they sprang up immediately, because they had no depth of soil. But after the sun rose, they were scorched; and because they had no root, they withered away. Others fell among the thorns, and the thorns came up and choked them out. But others fell on the good soil and yielded a crop, some a hundred, some sixty, and some thirty times as much. The one who has ears, let him hear"* (Matthew 13:3-9 NASB).

In this parable and explanation, Jesus is speaking about the seed of the Kingdom that gets sown in our hearts through encounters with His Word, His Spirit, and with His nature. When God speaks, it seeds our heart with Kingdom truth. Many times, the enemy will come in when a godly promise, prophetic vision, or purpose is sown in seed form within us and try sow seeds of fear and doubt that will compete with it. In this parable in Matthew 13, Jesus is explaining to the people how God the Father comes to sow seeds of promise in our hearts. These are seeds of truth and hope, of victory and joy, seeds of our destiny in Him, seeds of identity and breakthrough, and so much more. But in the midst of these Kingdom seeds being sown in our hearts, there are often other seeds that have been planted alongside them that start to compete for the same nutrients and the same resources as the seeds of God. The weeds of hardship grow and choke the life out of the Kingdom seed if we don't take time to tend to the condition of our hearts. The best thing we can do is to have our hearts unveiled before the Lord so that He can bring awareness of lies that are damaging that which He has said.

When the Holy Spirit begins to water the soil of our hearts, there are often other things that spring up alongside the seeds that have been planted. In this instance, the circumstances of the pandemic were watering a fear in my heart that a move of God could be quenched by external circumstances. The Lord was beginning to unlock an awareness in me that a great seed had been sown in the soil of my heart through this time of encounter with Him. I was seeing the beginnings of it springing up, and the enemy was showing up on the scene to see if he could abort the process God had started.

I could not control the pandemic, but I could control which seed grew by where I put my focus.

We are typically great at recognizing things when they are in full bloom and full expression. It's easy to see the value of an apple tree when there are apples all over it and we can taste the fruit. But can we recognize the potential in an apple seed before it ever becomes anything great? In one seed lies the DNA for thousands of apples and the potential for thousands of trees if it can be planted, watered, and tended to properly. I have heard people say that encounters are pointless if they don't change you, but I think we are missing some vitally important teaching around this subject. The lasting change happens for those who steward the gift given to them. The moment of powerful encounter awakens us and catalyzes us to see the Kingdom in full form, right in front of us. Encounter is the birthplace of walking in the ways of Jesus, but it does not stop with one moment; it is just the beginning.

If we saw encounters as seed, we would realize that there is more work to be done after than what is seen in that powerful moment. The encounter fills us with the grace and understanding that there is an incredible invitation in front of us to walk daily with the Holy Spirit, but that invitation must be accepted and stewarded in the tender heart of hunger and intimacy with the Lord. The work of the Spirit in us is to woo us to this place of yielding and giving Jesus everything, but we must accept the invitation.

To be awake in an awakening requires us to be able to live with eyes wide open to see things God is investing and doing in us. To recognize the power of His words in seed form, to see the great potential in the DNA of the seed, and to protect it with all we have.

WHERE TO FOCUS

I love how in the middle of this chapter in Matthew, before Jesus explains any of the parable, He stops and shares about our need to have ears to hear and eyes to see. In the midst of real life, we need spiritually attuned ears to hear and eyes to see what the Lord is saying and doing, and we need soft hearts toward Jesus to comprehend what is happening in the spirit realm because we live incredibly aware of what is happening in the natural. Instead of seeing our external circumstances, we need to focus on what the Holy Spirit is doing and partner with that.

The world was being shut down, everything that God had been doing outwardly in our environment had been brought to a screeching halt, and there was nothing that I could do about it in the natural. The lies of the enemy had started to encircle me, whispering in my ear, hoping to take root in my heart, but the moment I turned my heart to God I heard the truth He was speaking over my circumstance and it uprooted any lie that the enemy was trying to convince me of.

One simple sentence, breathed by God, "Hayley, be awake in an awakening," was what I needed to shift my perspective and realize that there was something happening that I could not yet see. His words gave me the reassurance that He was doing something, though I could not yet see it physically. It took faith to believe in the seeds that He had planted in my heart; it took commitment to stay present to His voice. I had to give time to Him—time in the Word, time in worship, time speaking with Him. As I gave Him my focus and affection, it produced fruit far greater than I could have ever imagined. This is the life lived in the spirit and not in the flesh. The life lived aware of the Holy Spirit and His work in us gives us the grace to enter in to the mysteries of God and His great work among us.

It honestly makes me wonder how many times God was stirring something in my heart but I hadn't had the ears to hear or the eyes to see the greater reality behind the circumstance. I don't feel shame about it, but I do let that wondering soften my heart and humble me, to remind me to remain connected to Him. One encounter, no matter how grand it is, cannot sustain you. The encounter is to invite you to greater awareness of our King and His Kingdom. Encountering the Holy Spirit makes you hungry for more of Jesus. It is our daily devotion to Jesus, His Word, and thus His heart that keeps us vigilant and cultivating His truth in our lives.

THE ENEMY IS A PROWLING LION

The enemy doesn't come to steal anything that isn't valuable—it wouldn't make sense. When a thief comes to steal, he goes after the most valuable things in the home.

The thief (satan) pursues the most powerful truths in our lives. He builds cases against the places that we were born to thrive and reveal God's glory. He is not creative. Like with Jesus in the wilderness, he comes to question our identity in Christ as sons and daughters and thus our authority over him. I have experienced this throughout my life. I have felt his lies try to choke the life out of the Word of the Lord. Why? Because he is terrified of a Bride that is awakened to the power of the Holy Spirit and the truth that we simply do not have to be enough on our own.

The enemy spent so much time trying to tell me that I wasn't enough, trying to make me qualify myself for what the Lord had spoken, because he is terrified of a people who recognize that God is more than enough for us. The enemy is terrified of a people who would rise in the power of the Spirit, understanding that they do not have to be sufficient in and of themselves but simply available to the one who is completely sufficient.

I had experienced for myself a great awakening, but the Lord never stops at one seed. His intention is to seed the world with the truth of His power and availability. He was wanting to expand my faith beyond an awakening for an individual, because He wants to awaken His people.

The lies of the enemy were invitations to become frantic and anxious or powerless and lulled to sleep into an apathetic state, but God was inviting me into a new reality. One where He was doing a great work behind the scenes, and my job was to rise in the power of His Spirit and believe Him, and partner in prayer with what He was doing. I am not sure if the prayer itself was making things move or if the prayer was moving something in me. I'm not sure it matters for me to understand whether I was moving or I was being moved. My role was simply to yield to His Word, and as I did the competing lies of the enemy were being uprooted and expelled from my heart and mind.

THE BONDAGE OF SHAME AND THE FREEDOM OF SALVATION

We cannot control circumstances or other people's choices, but we can control what we allow to grow and take root in our hearts. The challenge for some of us is letting the Lord into our hearts to do the work He needs to do. I spent a lot of time in my early Christian walk feeling like I needed to perform for approval. I thought I needed to do everything right to be loved by the Lord, so I would try to hide my heart from Him and tend to it myself. What I came to understand over the last few years is that God doesn't belittle us in our failure, but He releases the power of conviction, which can bring real transformation.

We often confuse conviction and shame. Shame is a thief. The Lord once told me that it is the "paralytic spirit." Shame says that when we do something bad, it indicates that we are bad people, corrupt at our core. This thinking leaves you feeling powerless to bring any transformation because you are the problem. Shame paralyzes us to feel powerful to see change. This is not the truth of the Gospel. When we believe we are powerless, we don't carry the necessary authority to steward our hearts before the Lord, and therefore we live with dualistic thinking. One moment we are in faith and the next we are in fear.

What we fail to understand is that we are not under a spirit of religion but have been saved by His great grace. When we are washed the blood of Jesus and receive it as the purchase for our sin, we become a new creation (see 2 Corinthians 5:17)—no longer under the law of sin and death but now under the covenant of His grace that leads to eternal life. We become adopted into God's family, and we receive His Holy Spirit who empowers us to live and think like God calls us to. In Jesus, God no longer identifies us by our sin but identifies us through the blood of Jesus as pure and set apart. No longer are we bound by our sin, but we are set free from sin and cleansed of all unrighteousness by the sacrifice of the pure and spotless Lamb of God.

When we don't understand the salvation of the Gospel, the narrative of shame is perpetuated in our lives. In shame, we become afraid to let God watch over our own hearts. We shy away from His conviction and the ownership for what is growing there because we are afraid of being disqualified. Rejection is one of the greatest fears humans face because we were designed to live in connection. The spirit of religion says we need to be perfect to be accepted, and so we reject our weakness and failure because we fear being worthless to the Lord. This is why shame paralyzes. Shame makes us feel like we are stuck in our own cycles, stuck by our history, by our pain, by the words spoken over us by others, and so much more. But this is not our portion. God has given us His Spirit to walk in our adoption as sons and daughters, and if we allow Him He will watch over our hearts and bring holy conviction to our souls.

THE HOLY SPIRIT, THE SEAL OF OUR SALVATION

Not only do we receive Jesus in the moment of salvation, but Jesus has given us the gift His Spirit, which He says:

> And it is God who establishes us with you in Christ, and has anointed us, and who has also put his seal on us and given us his Spirit in our hearts as a guarantee (2 Corinthians 1:21-22 ESV).

This shame-breaking Gospel of salvation is one that is not just given to us for a moment, but that powerful moment begins a work of liberation and sanctification in us for the rest of our days on this earth. The great work of salvation is sealed by the gift Jesus gave to us—His very own Spirit to dwell within us. The work of the Spirit within is what produces transformation in us—not our striving but our yielding to His work. The Spirit of God is called the "Holy" Spirit because He is absolutely pure and perfect and He walks with us in the day to day, filling us with His power to walk in purity and holiness as He is. We cannot become pure on our own; it is impossible. The cross is the place where our redemption and restoration to God's original design begins, but it does not stop there. When we receive the perfect sacrifice of Jesus, we are instantly made new in Him, but we are still living in a world full of contamination. That is why salvation comes with the gift of His Spirit. The Spirit of God is placed in our hearts to stand as a guarantee that we belong to Jesus and His Kingdom and that a life lived with Jesus is different (set apart) from the life lived by the world. We are in the world, but the Holy Spirit instructs us and empowers us to live a life not of this world but of the Kingdom. We need the Spirit to walk out a holy life. The journey of becoming like Jesus is one of surrender to the Spirit of God and the power of His conviction.

CONVICTION IS NOT SHAME

I used to be afraid of conviction because I connected it with shame. I saw God as angry with me, that He wanted to fix me so that He could love me. I had it all backward. When I encountered the Holy Spirit, the power of conviction came with this encounter. Instead of feeling God's disapproval of me, I felt His deep love for me and also the purity of His holiness. Conviction helps us see where we have made agreements and partnerships with lies in our lives that compete with the seeds God has sown. In conviction, we become awake to the things that are robbing us of freedom and the beauty of His life within us.

When the Holy Spirit started illuminating areas of my heart that were affected by believing lies, I saw clearly where I had gone wrong, where I lacked. God was not defining me by my lack or sin, He was inviting me to repent and have Him fill those spaces with His love. I felt the sorrow of my pride and the painful effects of finding safety in fear, but I also felt the welcome of His love to live in a new reality. Conviction would require me to give Him my lack, reservations, and fear, but in return He would fill me with Himself. Conviction was not there to tell me I was powerless; instead, it was there to remind me that in Christ I can walk in authority over the enemy and his ways.

The Holy Spirit is called the "Spirit of adoption" in Romans 8. The Spirit of God comes to awaken us to the reality that God first loved us and chose us well before we could choose Him. He calls us His children, which means we are loved irrespective of our actions. The transformation God wants to bring in our lives is not so that He can love us more but so that we can live in freedom and in full connection with Him. God will convict us of whatever is trying to stand in the way of His love for us. Conviction is a gift to the Christian because it leads us to repentance, and repentance clears that which hinders our connection with God.

God loves us extravagantly and His love is always available to us. He stands with arms wide open, welcoming every person to Him. He loves us whether we choose Him or not, but that does not mean we all live in the same connection to Him. God is love and God is holy. Though His love has no conditions, our connection with Him is based on our choosing. Because God is holy, He cannot live in union with sin because His nature is holy, and His nature never changes. When we choose sin, we violate our new nature in Jesus but also our connection to the Lord. We cannot live in sin and in intimate connection with the Holy Spirit. The Spirit is given to dwell in the believer, and He cannot reside where holiness is not cherished. God is always available to us, and He has made every provision in Jesus so that we never have to live in separation, but we must allow His conviction to live in our lives to live a life of purity.

It is the Holy Spirit who convicts us of our sin and furthermore convicts us of our new righteous nature that we have received in Jesus (see John 16:8). The Holy Spirit will bring a conviction that we can no longer partake in believing certain lies or finding comfort in unhealthy places. When we receive the Holy Spirit we receive Him, the Spirit of adoption. We break free from the mindset of shame so that we can step into full freedom of living with God in relationship.

In my encounter with the Holy Spirit, I found a joy in conviction and repentance. I felt the freedom of letting go of lies and hindrances so that I could run freely toward my upward call. I had spent so much time and energy believing that to be a good leader everyone needed to be happy with me. I was watering down the truth of the Lord in fear that people would be offended. In some ways, I believed that I could love people more than God could because I was adjusting what He was saying to me to try and keep people happy. Conviction and thus repentance broke me free from these mindsets and cast the weight of false responsibility from my shoulders and I was able to see clearly. I didn't stop loving people or honoring them; God loves people far more than I ever could. Allowing God's Spirit to bring conviction is welcoming freedom into our lives.

THE DISCIPLINE OF THE LORD IS NOT PUNISHMENT

The Holy Spirit convicts our hearts of sin and the lies we are believing so that we can step into the discipline of God. The discipline of God is not punishment. Punishment just deals with the action, but discipline deals with the heart. Punishment is for the benefit of the punisher; it tries to control and just make things "look better," while discipline is for the good of the person receiving it and it brings alignment to the purity of heart. In Hebrews 12:11, it says that His discipline leads to a fruit of "peaceful righteousness." This means that His discipline convicts us of anything that wants to rob us from living a life clean and pure and in perfect peace. His conviction comes with the fruit of peace. Conviction addresses anything that gets in the way of His love and nearness in our lives.

For us to be awake in an awakening requires full surrender to His hand and to His nature. We need to allow God to take full residence in our lives and give Him the full freedom to bring conviction in our hearts so that we can move uninhibited in the power of the Holy Spirit. It is the enemy that wants to shame us. The voice of shame sounds like: "How could you let this happen, Christian? You must be a really bad person or a really messed-up person to have that in your heart or in your mind." We have all heard this voice or voices like this. The voice of conviction, however, sounds like a voice that draws us closer to the holiness of God and reminds us that we have been made too clean and too pure to allow these things to exist in our lives when God lives within us.

As a parent, I discipline my children toward the destiny that God has called them to. Discipline is connected to prophetic vision. Discipline is not simply adjusting behaviors, but it is pointing our children toward who God calls them and what He calls them. It is adjusting mindsets and belief systems toward the way that God thinks. When my children's actions do not line up with the truth of who God calls them, I come with correction to redirect them toward the truth. It is only the truth the Lord speaks—Jesus, the way the truth and the life—that brings complete freedom.

When my children were toddlers they all went through the phase of using their hands to communicate. When frustrated with another sibling or one of us, they hit or pushed in aggression to show they were unhappy. When our firstborn started doing this, at first I would tell him that it was wrong and he was not allowed to behave that way, and it was true. However, it didn't cause much change in his behavior. One day I was asking the Lord what I should do about his hitting, and the Lord told me that next time he acted out I was to remind my son of the purpose that God created my son's hands for. The next time my son hit me, I sat him down on the bench in our bathroom. I first empathized with his frustrations and told him why it was not okay to hit despite these feelings, but then I went on to remind him that God had created his hands *for love*. I began to gently kiss each hand and tell him about how there is special love in his hands and how they are made for gentleness and kindness. I told him hands are not for hitting and started stroking my face and his with his hands and sharing about the tenderness in them. That was the day everything changed. As we started correcting the wrong behavior and reenforcing why God made our son's hands, something shifted in him, and after a few times of this the hitting stopped. Our son is now nearly eight years old, and I have seen the fruit of him understanding that the identity of his hands is wrapped up in the identity he has as a son of God. Hitting is a violation of his God design. When we know why we are made and understand the power of living in our God-given design, we live a life of conviction and purpose.

ALLOW HIM TO AWAKEN YOU

It is with sensitivity to the Holy Spirit, the person of great awakening, that we lay down everything that stands in the way of Him moving completely unhindered. Mindsets, belief systems, past experiences, unforgiveness, bitterness, offense all have to be laid at His feet so that the fullness of His Spirit, the fullness of the flow of His love cannot be hindered in our lives. To be awake in an awakening requires that we align ourselves to see as He sees, to hear what He is saying, and to carry in our hearts a desire to know what is in His heart. It is not relying on our ability that allows us to see or hear or know what He is doing, but it is our yieldedness to His Spirit that allows us to be awake to the things of Heaven.

Heaven is here; Heaven is available; it was made available when Jesus tore the veil in two and removed every separation between us and God. An awakening is when the Church rises in the awareness that God is here and He is fully available and He always has been. I believe we have been lulled to sleep, believing a lie of powerlessness or defeat, but the Spirit of God is rising among us and reminding His Bride that He is with us!

STAY AWAKE

Galatians 6:9 (NIV) says:

> *Let us not become weary in doing good, for at the proper time we will reap a harvest if we do not give up.*

Why do you think Paul is imploring the people in Galatia not to grow weary? Because we do. The enemy wants to wear us out by distracting us, by lying to us, and by exhausting us. There have been studies done by various marketing companies that say that the average American is exposed to 4,000 to 10,000 advertisements a day. That means that we are exposed to thousands of messages daily on who we should be, how we should act, and how we should think. These are competing seeds with the seeds of God.

For us to be awake in an awakening, we have to be vigilant to what God is saying and doing and keep our spirits aligned with the Holy Spirit and awakened to His reality and His movement day in and day out. It didn't take a lot for me to be realigned with the Lord, but simply giving myself completely in His presence and seeking His perspective in a place that I had fear. I had to disengage from worry and bring it to the feet of the Father, to invite His voice into a place in my heart. I needed to stop feeding the seed of fear and submit it to His nature and allow Him to speak and bring correction to mindsets that He did not have. This is what conviction is. It is the submission of my thoughts to His thoughts. It is the exchange of my fear for His perspective. It is allowing the Great Physician to do surgery on my heart and mind and take whatever is not of Him out of my life, no matter how comforting it is, because ultimately He is the only one who brings life.

Conviction is a gift. Discipline is a gift. It means that we have a Father who cares about us beyond what we even care about ourselves. It means that we don't belong to ourselves but we belong to Him. The Creator of the universe, the King of Glory has taken us as His possession and bought us with the highest price, the blood of Jesus. And His nature is love, it is freedom, it is fullness. We don't need to be afraid of conviction; we need it in our lives, for it produces the eternal fruit.

THE GIFT OF REPENTANCE

What follows holy conviction is a holy repentance. Repentance became one of the sweetest and most powerful gifts that I received in my encounter with the Holy Spirit. Repentance is the divine exchange of my thoughts for His thoughts, my yoke for His yoke. Repentance is such a powerful gift that we have been given from the Lord because it is the *Great Exchange*. Repentance is powered by the grace and mercy of God. His mercy is not just a one-time deal, but it is new every morning, available to us in any moment of turning.

In John 16:8-11 Jesus talks about the Holy Spirit and how He brings conviction of sin and righteousness.

> *And He, when He comes, will convict the world regarding sin, and righteousness, and judgment: regarding sin, because they do not believe in Me; and regarding righteousness, because I am going to the Father and you no longer are going to see Me; and regarding judgment, because the ruler of this world has been judged* (John 16:8-11 NASB).

When the conviction of the Holy Spirit comes upon us and we lean into repentance, He is welcomed to realign us with the way God thinks. Repentance recognizes inferior thinking and renews the mind to line up with the way God thinks about us and about things. It places His ways on the throne of our heart so that we can enter in to the greatness and glory of the Kingdom of our Lord. Repentance weeds the garden of competing seed in our lives and allows the seed of God to begin to flourish and thrive because it has nutrients available that it needs.

Repentance is a posture of humility. It allows us to remain at His feet, hanging on His every word, because we recognize that

He is the only one who gives life. And all of this is made possible by the power of the Holy Spirit in our lives.

In my encounter and many times after, I have wept deeply as I repented of things He brought conviction to. I remember realizing that the fear of man had been operating in my life because of pride. You see, I believed that by not stepping out in obedience I was keeping people happy; thus, I was loving them. I thought that being completely obedient to God would mean I wouldn't "love" people well because I would just be a walking offense. The problem with this thinking is that at the root of it I unknowingly believed that I loved people more than God. I had put my thoughts and ways above His and was relying on my own wisdom to navigate the tumultuous waters of culture and society. No matter how I adjusted myself, there was always another adjustment, exhausting me mentally and emotionally. Repenting of pride and that belief system allowed me to see God for the loving Father He is and for the power of the truth. It brought me freedom and relieved me from immense pressure. We were not designed to carry the weight of truth but to let Jesus define it and carry it, and we simply submit to it. The Holy Spirit convicts our heart of the truth, and truth is so loving because it is liberating.

We believe a lie in today's society that if it is the truth then it will feel good. To love someone isn't always going to make them feel wonderful. Think about this: your friend is sailing off on a cruise ship to embark on a wonderful holiday and a great adventure. You know they have spent the last four months saving, preparing, packing, laying out their plans, and you are heading to the dock to see them off. As they walk on the ship and are waving goodbye to you, you notice the ship has a giant hole beneath the surface that no one has seen. In that moment, you can feel your friend's excitement and anticipation; they have taken vacation time off of work and spent their savings on this trip. But no matter how excited they are and how disappointed they will be, it is not loving to let them sail away with a potential life threatening issue.

It is not kindness to ignore what God is saying, even if it is uncomfortable.

We have reframed love and made it into comfort. The truth is not always comfortable, but when it is given in the heart of love it is incredibly helpful and often lifesaving. My encounter with the Holy Spirit allowed me to see the root of these belief systems and brought me to a place where I could surrender them to the Lord and have Him reshape my thinking.

Repentance allows me to enter into God's lifesaving grace and walk in health and wholeness. It is not always comfortable, but it is incredibly good for me and I can feel His kindness in it. I don't want a life of comfort; I want a life full of purpose, hope, and joy. This is the work of repentance.

> I appeal to you therefore, brothers, by the mercies of God, to present your bodies as a living sacrifice, holy and acceptable to God, which is your spiritual worship. Do not be conformed to this world, but be transformed by the renewal of your mind, that by

*testing you may discern what is the will of God, what
is good and acceptable and perfect* (Romans 12:1-2
ESV).

Repentance renews our minds and allows us to think like God
thinks. It allows us to access God's mercy and grace and experience it. We don't need to be afraid of repentance, thinking that
it will feel bad for the rest of our lives. Repentance is painful for
a moment, but as we receive God's grace and mercy we begin to
feel the freedom it brings and thus the joy. God is victory; He is
hope, joy, freedom, and life. Repentance allows me to exchange
my sin and sorrow and receive His way of thinking.

The work of the Spirit of God in repentance is to illuminate
what is in our hearts so that anything that brings hindrance to
the fullness of His life is removed. When we repent of sin, the
blood of Jesus washes us clean and we become new and our
minds are transformed and renewed.

When we live a life aligned with the ways of God, we give full
access to the work of the Holy Spirit in us.

> *For to us God revealed them through the Spirit; for
> the Spirit searches all things, even the depths of God.
> For who among people knows the thoughts of a person
> except the spirit of the person that is in him? So also
> the thoughts of God no one knows, except the Spirit of
> God. Now we have not received the spirit of the world,
> but the Spirit who is from God, so that we may know
> the things freely given to us by God. We also speak*

these things, not in words taught by human wisdom, but in those taught by the Spirit, combining spiritual thoughts with spiritual words.

But a natural person does not accept the things of the Spirit of God, for they are foolishness to him; and he cannot understand them, because they are spiritually discerned. But the one who is spiritual discerns all things, yet he himself is discerned by no one. For who has known the mind of the Lord, that he will instruct Him? But we have the mind of Christ (1 Corinthians 2:10-16 NASB).

CHAPTER 4

THE SURRENDERED LIFE

HOLY SPIRIT MAKES US HUNGRY FOR MORE OF JESUS

I am often around believers who are just so hungry for more of the Lord. When you have tasted His goodness and His nature, you cannot be satisfied by anything other than all of Him. I've seen desperation turn to a challenging frustration in people and myself at times. The tension of gratitude (thanks for what has happened) and desire (longing for more in the future) is not an easy one to navigate, but I have realized this frustration can actually be a holy invitation from the Lord if we can posture our hearts and thoughts toward His abundance instead of fear of lack. When we adopt the posture of a child toward the Kingdom of God, frustration is an invitation to know Him more, to experience a new facet of His glory, and go deeper into the Lord's heart.

The reality is that hunger for God in your life is the very evidence of the work of the Holy Spirit in you. When I began to realize that the deep hunger and tension I felt was in fact the work of the Spirit making room for me to know Jesus, my frustration turned into anticipation and gratitude. I started to bless the hunger and declare I was about to know Jesus in a more profound way. This posture of anticipation and gratitude was the very thing I needed to receive what He had prepared. There is no desire the Holy Spirit would put in your heart that He doesn't want to fill with Jesus. When the Holy Spirit is welcomed to work in our life and we invest in our connection with Him, He begins to make room in our heart to desire to know and experience God in greater measure.

BECOMING AWARE OF THE WORK OF THE HOLY SPIRIT

Something I have heard Bill Johnson say very often about hunger in the Kingdom is that it is the opposite of hunger in the natural. In the natural, you get hungry when you don't eat, but in the Kingdom you get hungry by eating. The more of God we experience, the more of His Word we consume, and the more we desire to know and experience Jesus. There have been many times I have told people they need to get hungry for God, and honestly it was the truth. There can be apathy that creeps into our lives when we stop eating from the table of the Lord. We become satisfied when we stop seeking after Him. Sometimes this happens because of disappointments in our lives or because of pain. Sometimes it simply happens because we are tired, overwhelmed, and distracted by the challenges in life. The one that concerns me the most is when we move into a space where we become satisfied with what we know because of what we have experienced and we become content with a measure of Him without hungering for His fullness.

At times I have found in myself this frustration with where we are as a body. In those moments, I can choose to correct and press on those around me to get hungry, and at times it is needed, but it has not proved to be the most effective way to lead people into powerful encounters with the Lord.

To lead others is not to simply state what we see is not happening but to discern what God is doing to woo them into connection with Him. I have recognized that when we focus on our lack, that is where we will invest our faith, and where we invest our faith, we bear fruit. Helping people to posture themselves to become aware of the great mercy of God that has been poured out for us in Jesus and the availability of the Holy Spirit begins to invite them to invest their faith in what is available rather than in what is not happening. Awakening the hearts of believers to the move of the Spirit and the desire of God to meet with them breaks down the walls of discouragement and reminds us that He is already inviting us—we just need to recognize and accept.

Many people think they need to be special or chosen to experience friendship with God, but the reality is that Jesus made a way for all of us to come to the Father. It is in the surrender of our heart to the lordship of Jesus and the giving of ourselves to the work of the Holy Spirit in our lives that we step into this wonderful union with Him. The Spirit is constantly at work in our lives preparing us, healing us, and stirring us to receive and encounter the Lord. When we turn our attention from lack and into His marvelous mercy and availability, we submit ourselves to His work in our lives. We move from striving to surrender and feeling peace in our dependence on Him.

Recognizing and becoming grateful for the work of the Holy Spirit in our lives funnels our attention toward the work of God in us. Taking our eyes off of ourselves and setting them on His moving and outpouring attaches our faith to His ways, and it is in this place we see the increase of His presence manifest in and through us. If you are hungry for more of God, right there is the evidence of the Holy Spirit working in your life. In hunger we can look at what is missing or we can look to the one who is sufficient. Our hunger for more of God could only come from the work of the Spirit in our lives. It is, after all, His pleasure to glorify and reveal Jesus to us. Turn your eyes from the lack in your hunger and fix your eyes on His presence. Invite Him to fill you, submit your lack to His sufficiency, and offer yourself as a living sacrifice. Here in this place He will meet you and fill you to overflowing.

SURRENDER: THE BIRTHPLACE OF ENCOUNTER WITH GOD

So many people desire to encounter the Holy Spirit, to know God in a powerful and profound way, and I tell you, God desires it even more than we do. But I have found the birthplace of encounter with the Holy Spirit is not in our striving but in complete surrender. When we talk about striving, I am talking about that place where we become focused on ourselves, on what is not happening and what we are or aren't doing. Striving for God in our flesh is not always a bad thing; it's just not the most powerful action we can take to receive Him.

If you were in a committed relationship and you recognized that you were living disconnected, I am sure there would be a measure of striving to move toward the heart of your loved one. Often those initial attempts come from a mindset of lack and fear, and when we muddle fear and love into the same agenda it gets complex and exhausting. Our overworking to solve the issue produces less than the work of us surrendering and becoming soft toward love. Surrender is not passive; I believe it is a far deeper work than striving is, and it produces a far deeper result. Surrender is us giving ourselves to a vulnerable "weak feeling" place of laying down and putting trust in the other we are moving toward.

The Holy Spirit is often described in a way that tells us that He is sensitive. When the Holy Spirit rested on Jesus, He did so in the form of a dove, an animal that would not rest in a restless place. Though God doesn't scorn our striving, just as a parent would not reject their child for crying out for their affection or attention, it is in the place of surrender we truly make an altar for God to rest upon.

As a mother, when my child strives for my attention I do my best to give it to them, to meet their need, and to pour my love out on them. I often find, however, their striving is busy and noisy and I am not sure my love always gets to sink in as deeply as I would love it to. And then there are the moments when they come quietly and tenderly toward me, when they crawl up on my lap and nestle into my arms. Those are the quiet, yielded moments I am able to speak into deep places of their hearts in a way I can't when they are trying to prove themselves. The posture of surrender requires my children to trust that I will be soft with them in return. If this is what earthly parents do, how much more is our heavenly Father seeking ways to pour His love and affection out on us. Surrender can feel weak, quiet, and vulnerable, but it is the posture of invitation.

HIS STRENGTH IN OUR WEAKNESS

To walk in true surrender requires obedience, and obedience is a powerful attitude that allows the Lord to flow uninhibited in us and through us. Obedience is a posture of truly laying ourselves and our agenda down in the same way Christ did for us. It is a yielding of self-will and becoming completely dependent on the will of God for us to function. This obedient and yielded posture allows us to become that portal for His power to flow. This is why weakness is so powerful.

> But he said to me, "My grace is sufficient for you, for my power is made perfect in weakness." Therefore I will boast all the more gladly about my weaknesses, so that Christ's power may rest on me (2 Corinthians 12:9 NIV).

Our weakness is often a place we see the move of the Spirit because it is the place His power can flow uninhibited and it is obvious that it is Him at work. Our weakness is a place we are overtly aware that we need help in and so we often cry out to God from that place. Weakness is a yielded, surrendered place—it has no strength to strive. When we get to the end of our rope, it is where God really can work because we get out of our own way.

OBEDIENCE OVER SACRIFICE

When the fear of man was in operation in my life, I had two masters. I was trying my best to follow and obey God, giving as much of myself as I could give, but I had empowered the fear of man to speak loudly and influence my obedience. When there is more than one master in our lives, we are unable to live a life of complete obedience and surrender because we are doing the dance of yielding between multiple voices. On one hand, I had the voice of Jesus asking me to take risks and follow Him completely, but I had another voice fearing the outcome if I did.

In 1 Samuel 15, Samuel has anointed Saul as king, and the first instruction from the Lord is for Saul to completely destroy the Amalekites and everything that belongs to them. This is quite an intense story, but it paints a picture of what it means to have a yielded heart. The Lord looks for a heart that will have no other gods, no other competition with His voice because He knows it is the only way to live in freedom. In the story of 1 Samuel 15, Saul responds at that moment and gathers the people of God to do as God had commanded. But we see that Saul doesn't completely follow through with the command. He does mostly as instructed, but he preserves the life of King Agag and the choice livestock of the people.

The Lord deeply regrets making Saul king and sends Samuel to confront him. In this confrontation, Saul declares that he kept the choice livestock to offer to the Lord as a sacrifice, and Samuel responds with something profound that many of us have heard quoted. He says God desires obedience over sacrifice (see 1 Samuel 15:22).

I want to pause for a moment and think about this statement. God desires obedience over sacrifice. God was the one who came up with the idea of making sacrifices, but that was only introduced after man fell. This passage in 1 Samuel 15:22 is where we see what the heart of God has been from the beginning. Obedience is what God desires, because obedience is a choice by us to live in oneness and union with Him. The posture of obedience is one of complete trust in the Lord and His nature. Sacrifice came from us choosing independence from His ways and was introduced in our rebellion to the Lord. Though sacrifice was deemed acceptable for sin, it has never been what God desired. Jesus became the ultimate sacrifice so that we would never have to live a life of duality ever again.

In this story, Saul later admits that he was in fact afraid of his people and made the choice to not obey God because he didn't want to make the people unhappy, fearing what they might do. Saul was trying to serve two masters, God and his people, and was making excuses of sacrifice because he could not be truly obedient with the fear of man operating in his life. The fear of man robs us of a wholehearted yes to God. When we have the fear of man enthroned on our lives, we live like a wave tossed back and forth in the ocean—one moment walking in great faith and the next second guessing our every move in fear we would be rejected or disapproved of. This limits the work of the Holy Spirit and the freedom He brings in our lives in every way.

When God created Adam and Eve, they had complete freedom and were walking in authority over everything created. In this place of complete freedom, they were asked one thing—to obey God and not eat from the fruit of the tree of the knowledge of good and evil. So long as they lived in obedience to their covenant with God, they would have free reign over everything and full access to God without restriction. But when they disobeyed God, sin was introduced and they became separate from God. The life of obedience and love was now defiled by sin, and distance was created between them and their holy God. Thus, sacrifice was introduced into their relationship. Sacrifice became the offering that filled the gap that rebellion created, and it only exists in a world where we aren't living wholly before God and God alone. When we allow more than one voice to contribute to the leadership of our lives, we introduce a life of sacrifice into our existence. The life of sacrifice is one in which we constantly feel the cost of saying yes to God because we are so aware of the world and what we are saying no to. The thoughts and opinions of the world shout at us from all directions, vying for our allegiance, telling us what we are giving up and the cost of each decision. The life that lives in full obedience has killed every option to listen to those who are shouting because Jesus has taken the first and only place in their lives and a yes to Him is better than a thousand elsewhere.

In my life, so long as the fear of man was allowed to operate and speak into my choices and destiny, I would have to live a life of sacrifice and not wholehearted obedience. Though I deeply desired to live in complete obedience, I was torn between quick obedience and negotiating with God and fear.

Every time I would get up to speak and especially after I was done, I would find myself overwhelmed and negotiating with God about my security of heart and future. I would feel this amazing passion and fire when I would teach—I would sense the Lord near, and I would often feel like I was doing what I was born to do—and in the very next breath my mind would be flooded with an intense fear of failure, saying things like, "This is too much, it's not worth it, I never want to do this again." I was ready to abandon what He created me for because of the power fear had in my life. Instead of surrendering, I thought my best option was to run from what felt so painful and impossible.

We must understand this, the enemy is terrified of the church discovering the truth of the Holy Spirit and who He is to us. Satan is terrified of a Bride empowered by the King himself. He knows that prophecy from Genesis 3:15—that he will bruise our heel but the seed of the woman, Jesus, will crush his head. Jesus is the one who will crush the head of the enemy, and He has given us His Spirit to live and dwell within us. The Spirit of God is looking for a life that is fully surrendered through which to flow freely and powerfully to destroy the works of the enemy and demonstrate His glorious power, so the world will know the King lives and reigns. Humans are the only creation that have been given the authority in Jesus to crush satan underneath our feet, but we have to disempower the lies that the enemy is feeding us. We do this by cutting off the power of the enemy's voice and giving ourselves to completely obeying the voice of God. We can only obey by the power of the Spirit.

In the life of sacrifice, we have the option to choose who we obey in the moment, but in the life lived in obedience we have relegated ourselves to one thing—what He is asking. When we live in full surrender to the Lord we cut off the appetite for anything other than Jesus. Now, instead of living in sacrifice, we ourselves become the sacrifice (the offering). Fire always falls on the offering. Our lives of obedience and surrender are like the "sweet savor" offerings in Leviticus. Our lives laid down in obedience are not to pay for sin; Jesus did this once and for all.

He was the pure spotless lamb that paid our penalty of death. We are the ones who bring an offering of choice, devotion, and worship, and only we can give that to Him because God gave us the choice. When we destroy the influence of the enemy in our lives and in faith we lay down that which we have found comfort in (that is not Him), striving ceases and we become a resting place for the Dove.

Living in a constant state of sacrifice is an exhausting way to live. In one moment standing on what God is saying and then doubting the next moment—the constant back and forth left me rattled and tired. The slave driver of the fear of man demands we scurry around working hard for every opinion and point of view to be in agreement. Constantly aware of what we are laying down, seeing the price we are paying, and moment by moment fighting for our attention to be on the truth. The life of sacrifice is tiring, but no matter how tired we get we cannot rest because there is more to do and more people to please. I was exhausted and burned out fighting for my focus. Was I living a radical life fully given to Jesus or was I going to shrink back and hide because I didn't want to fail? When I finally was able to surrender, that was the birthplace of experiencing the power of God in a way I could never manufacture.

Zechariah 4:6 (NASB) says:

> *Then he said to me, "This is the word of the Lord to Zerubbabel, saying, 'Not by might nor by power, but by My Spirit,' says the Lord of armies."*

When we choose the life of obedience, we choose to surrender our might and our strength, and we usher the Holy Spirit to flow through our lives uninhibited. In the surrender of our strength is where we meet the greatest power in the world—the Spirit of God.

LAYING DOWN OUR SELF-CONSTRUCTED SHIELDS

I have often been asked, "What does it mean to lay down the shield of the fear of man?"

To lay down a shield is to lay down our protection. In battle, a shield is there to block the weapons of the enemy that seek to destroy us. When I say I used the "fear of man" as my shield, I mean that it became how I protected myself from what I feared. I feared failing because somewhere in my life I believed the lie that I am worthless if I fail people. And so, to protect myself from what I feared, I picked up people pleasing (fear of man) to shield myself from pain. I noticed at times I would use my discernment to discern who was disapproving or disconnected from what I was doing or saying as a leader, and I would find ways to overwork and pursue what would maybe bring them into connection more. Other times, I would dilute the intensity of what I felt the Lord was saying or I would over apologize for anything that felt harder to hear. All of these things would actually produce more approval from people, but there was no real life in it for me.

In Ephesians 6, Paul teaches about the armor of God, and in that is the shield of faith. Faith in God is what shields us from the fiery arrows of the enemy that purpose to wound us and take us out. We all desire to have the shield of faith as our shield, but it is not always the reality we live in. In my mind, I saw a picture of a shield that was comprised of all the ideologies and worldly wisdom that I had crafted around me in order to keep me from stepping outside of the boundaries society had told me I had to stay in. I used to constantly feel like I was either too much or not enough, but never just right. The voice of the fear of man would constantly be telling me to hold myself back, keep quiet, or tame the passion I felt. This fear in my life tried to keep my expression of the Gospel tame and thus to keep myself tame because the way God made me seemed too fiery. I would feel embarrassed when I let my passion out, feeling like it was too much for people and that they wouldn't like me or would be offended by my zeal.

I would shield myself with worldly wisdom on how I could be quieter or less intense. On top of feeling like I was too much, I also felt like I was too soft and too sensitive (not enough). So just when I held myself back "enough," when I didn't share the passion that was burning inside of me for the Lord, I would be hit with the other side. This fear was that my emotions were too strong, that when I cried and was soft people wouldn't know what to do with me, and the list goes on and on. No matter how much I adjusted myself or came up with new ways to shield myself, it was never going to be enough.

Perhaps you do not have the fear of man in the same way I felt it. Maybe it's insecurity or the fear of rejection. I know each of us have dealt with fear or insecurity trying to speak to us in some way, shape, or form, but that voice is just the voice of the thief and the liar. The antidote for this voice is not another tool or piece of advice, but it is in the voice of God the Father and the identity He speaks over us. It is in the fear of the Lord and how He thinks about us that we truly become free. God has written us a love letter revealing His ways and His heart to us in His Word. A Father who so loved us that He made a way to be with us, no matter how far we fell or the cost for Him. Not only did He redeem us through His sacrifice for us, but He then breathed the life breath of His Spirit into us and empowered us with Himself—that is how much He loves us and believes in us. Fear of the Lord is connected to us living a life in absolute awe and wonder of His greatness, power, and majesty, with only His opinion weighing in at the end of the day.

TRUSTING THE LORD

For us to allow the voice of God to shape every part of our lives, it means that we have to yield our understanding to Him.

Trust in the Lord with all your heart and do not lean on your own understanding. In all your ways acknowledge Him, and He will make your paths straight (Proverbs 3:5-6 NASB).

Too often we have built constructs of our own understanding to try and protect ourselves from the pain or trauma in our history and our past. The Lord is asking for us to lay down our defense mechanisms and surrender our ways to His. Something I have realized is that the fear of man centers on us. The focus is on our lack, our excess, our greatness or failure. The shield of the fear of man causes us to live a life focused on us. The fear of God and the shield of faith in God looks at His ability and His great love for us. It is not that we don't factor in the equation; it is just that we are not the source—Jesus is. Although tools I have learned have helped me become aware of areas, I need God to fill in my life, I have never found freedom in my own ideas. It is the life lived fully surrendered to Jesus that truly experiences complete freedom. When we let go of our own understanding and ways and trust in the Lord, we enter the "God-life." For His ways are not our ways; they are higher than ours. It's not that the Lord does not care about our past or our history. In fact, it is the opposite. He is Emmanuel, God with us, through all of our pain and our trials. He never leaves us, nor does He forsake us. He doesn't want us to simply cast aside our experience, but He wants us to bring it to His feet so that He can make the final determination. Many times, the thief wants to have the final say on a circumstance, but God says, "Bring it to Me, lay it at My feet, I alone have the authority to speak life, truth, and freedom over you and transform it by My grace." Every place that the enemy wants to hold you back, wants to rob from your life, God says, "I will pour My Spirit out upon you, and I will change the narrative that your circumstances have spoken."

It is only in trust that we can experience full surrender. We cannot give to the Lord what we will not trust Him with. As we look at His nature, faithfulness, goodness, everlasting kindness, and His pursuit of us we realize we are living in a mercy moment. It is by His mercy that we surrender (see Romans 12:1), and it is in surrender that we begin to experience the power of the Holy Spirit flowing through our lives. Each of us who are in Christ has received the Holy Spirit as the seal of our salvation (see Ephesians 1:13), we receive the Spirit the day we receive Jesus as our Savior. This means that He lives and dwells in us as our wonderful counselor, our helper, or comforter, and the one who reveals and glorifies Jesus. The Holy Spirit is fully available to us every minute of every day, withholding nothing from us and He is there from the point of our salvation in Jesus.

While all believers have the Holy Spirit from the day of salvation, from my experience and understanding of Scripture I believe that there is a difference between having the Holy Spirit dwell within you than it is experiencing His power and authority flow through your life to release and demonstrate the Kingdom here on earth.

Though the Spirit is available to every believer if we want to demonstrate the Kingdom, we need to posture ourselves to receive and access the power of the Spirit so that He may flow uninhibited through our beings. This kind of living requires us to surrender every construct or argument that would limit His moving in our lives and put all our trust in the Lord.

Jesus is the one who baptizes us in the Holy Spirit. John declared that his baptism is one of water and repentance but Jesus was coming to baptize us in the Holy Spirit and fire (see Matthew 3:11). And it was Jesus who instructed His disciples to wait in the upper room until they were filled with the Holy Spirit and clothed with His power. The waiting for the outpouring of the Spirit demonstrated complete trust and surrender to the plans of Jesus; confined to one space and place waiting on the instructions Jesus had given them, believing for something they had no grid for, to take place. When the Spirit was poured out upon those waiting in the upper room, they were clothed in power and filled with boldness, and the Church of Jesus was born. This baptism however did not stop there, the Bible clearly shows us that we are to live a life in surrender to God and continually filled with His Holy Spirit to carry out the Gospel mandate (see Acts 4:8; Acts 13:9-10; Acts 13:52). This posture of waiting in the upper room is to be the daily posture of our hearts, living in dependence on His words and hunger for Him to move mightily in and through us. I learned this so profoundly in my six-week encounter with God. Yes, I had been baptized in the Holy Spirit as a youth but this fresh infilling I received reminded me that this was the Christian way of life. We were created to host the Holy Spirit so that our life is a demonstration of Spirit and power here on earth by living in surrender and dependence on Him daily (see 1 Corinthians 2:4). This encounter that I experienced taught me this and changed my way of living. It taught me that I could live each day in intimate connection and fully filled by God's Spirit so that I might carry His power and bring His Kingdom here on earth. When my striving and fight for freedom turned to surrender and dependence, I was able to become a living sacrifice for God's holy fire.

The Holy Spirit does not compete and seldom pushes His way through, He waits patiently for us to make space and invite Him to move and operate in our lives.

POOR IN SPIRIT

Blessed are the poor in spirit, for theirs is the kingdom of heaven (Matthew 5:3 NASB).

To be poor in spirit means that I recognize that I cannot add anything to God no matter what I bring or how hard I try. The enemy has been attempting to drive a narrative in culture that has painted a picture of God as a demanding control freak who wants to run our lives because He has some over inflated ego He needs to feed. Other times, I see people feeling like God is asking things of us because He needs our things to function. This is completely opposite from the truth. God doesn't need anything from us to be God; He is completely sufficient in and of Himself. He doesn't need my money, nor my voice; He doesn't need my ministry or my call to be any greater than He is right now. God is the greatest in every way. He is greater than we can imagine, what we know, and what we have experienced. He does not need anything more from us, but because He is love He desires to do it with us. His nature being love and His choice to live in connection with us means that He has chosen to wait for our welcome. Love cannot violate choice because then it would not be love; love can only be true where there is an option. That is why there was the other tree in the garden.

God doesn't want us because He needs us; He wants our invitation because He loves us and has chosen for His glory to be made manifest in our connection to Him. Everything God asks of us is not to add to Him, but it adds to us. He will only ask for what is stealing our attention and affection from Him and thus the abundant life that He paid for us to live.

When I recognized that I was poor in spirit without Him, that I did not have enough in and of myself, I was able to be introduced to the one who is sufficient. This is the best news I could have heard. God doesn't need me to be amazing to love me or flow through me; He just wants all of me, as I am. I had spent so much time trying to be "enough" for God and people, and in this powerful truth I realized I didn't need to be sufficient—He was and He is.

The world says that you need to be strong, you need to be bold, and you need to have it all together in order to walk out the destiny on your life. The world says that in order to get somewhere in life you need to help yourself, that you are the problem and therefore you are the solution. But the Gospel says that Jesus helps the helpless, that He came while we were still sinners (see Romans 5:8). In Psalm 105 we are told that we should call on the name of the Lord when we are in a time of trouble and He will deliver us. He calls Himself our rescuer, our provider, our healer, and our shield. Of course, we can't just sit back and float into the distance; we need to respond, but we certainly are not the first to make the move. Our job is not to be the initiator but to respond to His invitation and say yes to partner with God. He has made the first move already, and we get to bring ourselves to Him as we are and partner from a weak place with a simple, obedient, faithful "yes."

THE MUSTARD SEED RESPONSE

Whenever the Word of God speaks about our contribution, we begin to realize that it's very small in comparison to the outcome, but what we have is all He is asking for. Our contribution is the five loaves and two fish that end up feeding five thousand. It's the faith the size of a mustard seed that ends up moving the mountain. The math of this equation is miraculous. Our yes plus God's yes equals billions. When we bring our one and He adds Himself it becomes exponential in increase—it is just supernatural. But what else would a wonderfully supernatural God do? We spend so much time trying to be "all" that we forget we just need to fulfill the part we have been given and offer what we have with a grateful heart, and He will partner with us and fill every void.

One of the greatest things that I discovered in my encounter was that I didn't need to be enough. I understand what we are saying when we tell people that they are enough. I know that we are saying that you aren't discounted, and I fully believe in that. We are incredibly valuable to the Lord and we are enough for Him. But I was believing that I needed to figure out how I could be enough for God and everyone on my own, like I was trying to become something so that He could be with me. We unintentionally place ourselves as the hinge of the story, that everything rests on us. I thought that if I don't get it right then I was going to miss it.

I am not at the center of the story; Christ is at the center of the story. Jesus isn't the addition to my life, a stepping stone toward my destiny. Jesus is at the center of this powerful story, and He invites me into His story. It is incredibly liberating when we let go of our own narrative and we come into Jesus's story. In Jesus's story, He is the one who is in charge; He is the one who is navigating and managing it all. My role is not to figure it out or plan it all but simply to give myself to Him and partner in the work He has begun. My yieldedness and obedience to Him allows me to move with Him unhindered and watch Him finish the work He starts.

> *For I am confident of this very thing, that He who began a good work among you will complete it by the day of Christ Jesus* (Philippians 1:6 NASB).

My job is not to figure out how Jesus will complete the story but to surrender my life to Him and all of my understanding and allow the work of the Holy Spirit in me to accomplish everything the Father has spoken. When I live a life of surrender to the will of God and to what is in His heart, I allow the free-flowing power of the Holy Spirit to move through me and rest upon my life. This is where impossibilities become possible.

THE ANOINTING OF THE HOLY SPIRIT

I've heard it said many times that "this person is anointed." I believe when we are saying that we are identifying a life that has been surrendered to the Lord and has become a place that the Holy Spirit can rest upon. The anointing is not a thing or a tool, it is a Person—the Holy Spirit.

A life lived in sacrifice and striving is a life with anxiety and lacks peace. Jesus is called the Prince of Peace. We see in Matthew 3 how Jesus allowed the dove to rest on His shoulders as He carried peace. This is a picture of someone who is rooted in their identity in the Lord and is living in full obedience. Philippians 2 talks about the obedience that Jesus chose to walk in even unto death on the cross. When Jesus chose to take on flesh, He laid Himself down fully and allowed the Father's will to become completely manifest in His life. Jesus was demonstrating to us what a life lived in surrender could look like. The Holy Spirit had found His resting place on the life of Jesus in such a powerful way that miracles, signs, and wonders followed Him everywhere He went. A life lived in full obedience and surrender to the Lord welcomes the resting of the Dove, the Holy Spirit.

If it is not by might nor by power but by the Spirit, then we need the power of the Holy Spirit to be resting on our lives in order to see the power and might of the Kingdom manifest in this world. We cannot live the supernatural life without the supernatural empowerment of the Spirit of God. There are no gifts of the Spirit without the Holy Spirit. There is no anointing without the Holy Spirit. When we place Jesus in the center and we get into His story, we enter into a story of full surrender and incredible power of the Spirit of God. We don't want to simply give the world a Gospel of form, but a Gospel of the transformational power of God. It is the life transformed by the power of God that truly transforms the world.

A lot of people talk about how we're going to change the world, and I think it's wonderful because God truly wants us to. But when we forget about who changes the world, we get caught up in what we are doing and not what the Lord is doing. This is not diminishing the part we play but should encourage us to remember who is in charge and whose power we are walking in.

THE HOLY SPIRIT WILL HELP YOU

Surrender is not supposed to be a complicated formula that is unattainable for most people. Surrender is simple because it is empowered by the Holy Spirit. When we bring what we have to the Holy Spirit and invite Him in to help us, He releases grace on our lives so that we can say yes to Him. Many people feel like they don't have enough faith. Well, I have great news for you, the Holy Spirit is the giver of the gift of faith. If you don't know how to surrender yourself, you can invite the Holy Spirit to come and help you, and He will meet you.

Surrender is what allows us to obey. When we say yes to the invitation of God, we have to let go of the things that hold us back. Many people think correction is punishment; it is a moment when they find out that they are wrong or bad. But true discipline is an invitation to His ways. When we turn from a life of sacrifice and surrender to Him and start living a life of obedience, we are able to receive the freedom He paid for. This isn't about how bad we are or how wrong we are; this is about how good He is and how powerful He is. In surrender, we exchange our ways for His and we get to live in the ways of the Kingdom and not of this world.

QUICK OBEDIENCE

When we practice small and quick obedience, it becomes easier to say yes in the bigger, more costly moments. I've heard it said that delayed obedience is disobedience. An example of that is me as a mother asking my children to go brush their teeth. They may say yes, but often they don't turn the television off, or they go and wander into their rooms and start playing a game. They have the intention of eventually brushing their teeth, but I am not asking them to do it by the next day, I am saying, "Now is the time to brush your teeth." There have been times in my life the Lord has asked me to do something, and I have every intention of doing it one day, but just not today. Sometimes we are waiting for a day when we feel better, more equipped, more powerful, or more mature, but the Lord isn't asking for one day—He is asking for today. And if He is asking now, He is going to fill all the gaps.

When we delay, we delay experiencing the power and grace that He is offering us. When we wait to feel strong, we deny the experience of His power in us. Surrender and immediate obedience allow Him to work wonders in our lives and His authority to flow through us. I started noticing as I would walk in small and quick obedience, I began to feel more confident in the Lord and His power instead of my own. Quick obedience caused me to have no other option but to rely on Him in all things and thus discover that He is more wonderful and more powerful than I could conceive. Quick obedience allows us to experience Him in ways that we need to but haven't been able to will ourselves to. Small and consistent steps of quick obedience have led me to greater and quicker obedience to Jesus because it has refined me. In this season I find myself way out of my depth, doing things far beyond my capabilities. I find incredible comfort that I am His and that the Lord is with me. At times I recognize I am walking on water and I feel afraid. There are times when I want to limit my output and pull back to self-protect, but then I remember that will not produce peace, only a ceiling of limitation. When I remember that all I need to do is lock eyes with Jesus and yield to the work of the Holy Spirit in me, I receive the courage I need to say "yes" once more. He is powerful enough, strong enough, loving enough, wise enough, and all I am is a vessel of love to make His glory manifest. This is who we are, and simple and quick obedience allows us to step into this reality.

As we close this chapter, I want to invite you to pray this prayer for surrender with me:

> God, I do not know how to fully surrender to You on my own, but You have given me the gift of Your Holy Spirit to help me and lead me, and I receive Him. I invite You, Lord to come and show me Your ways— teach me to see things like You see them. Holy Spirit, will You help me surrender everything to Jesus? Will You help me surrender my defense mechanisms and the things that have become places of constant sacrifice in my life? Lord, I repent of putting my trust in other constructs and I put my trust completely in You. Jesus, I entrust my life to You and ask for Your Spirit to come and work in me so that the will of God would be done in my life. Holy Spirit, would You reveal Jesus to me? Would You show me His nature so that I may know Him? Holy Spirit, I need You. I desire to have You operate in fullness in my life.

> Jesus, I thank You that You made a way for me to receive the fullness of what God has for me because of Your precious blood. I receive Your blood as a sacrifice for my sin. It is more than enough for me to enter into

the story that You have written for me. Jesus, I get out of the preoccupation with my own story, and I get into Your story. I recognize I do not have what it takes in and of myself, but You have chosen me and You are more than enough. You are more than sufficient and You fill me with Your Presence. I receive the truth that You are sufficient for me, that Your grace is enough in my weakness. I love You, Jesus. Holy Spirit, would You reveal the thoughts of the Father and the love of Jesus to me so that I can love Him more and thus love others.

Holy Spirit, let my surrender to You become a resting place for You so that the power of God flows through my life to bring God's Kingdom here on earth. I make myself completely available to You and offer myself as a living sacrifice to you, Jesus. Set my life ablaze for the sake of Your name, by the power of Your Spirit. Amen.

CHAPTER 5

THE TEMPLE OF THE HOLY SPIRIT

ALLOWING THE TRUTH TO BECOME PERSONAL

In this divine season of encounter, I found myself undone by repentance for how I approached the Holy Spirit. My entire being was being awakened to the reality that I myself was the temple of the Holy Spirit. I have heard this said many times—too many to count, in fact. In my brain, I had the knowledge of this truth, and if you had asked me prior to this powerful touch from God I would have quoted the Scripture in 1 Corinthians 6:19. But this is one of the many reasons why we need to encounter God, why we need to collide with the power of the Holy Spirit. We need to be awakened on the inside, at the core of our being, to enter into realities we are cognitively aware of but experientially disconnected from.

John 8:32 (NASB) says that *"you will know the truth, and the truth will set you free."* In this passage, Jesus is speaking to a system that had a lot of knowledge but failed to recognize Him as the Messiah. He was inviting them into an experience with a reality that they knew a lot about and had been waiting for. Many who had heard the prophecies of the coming Messiah and were waiting for Him did not actually receive Jesus and thus did not experience the liberation they were waiting for. To truly know something means that I have not simply heard and agreed with the word, but I have experientially entered into the truth by applying it in my day-to-day life.

During this life-changing shaking of the Spirit of God, I would weep uncontrollably under the weight of the Holy Spirit's resting. A deep repentance had come over me as things I knew mentally became a living, breathing reality. I had unknowingly depersonalized so much by being satisfied with knowledge of God but not pursuing a daily meeting and communion with Him. I would find myself sobbing on the floor saying to the Lord, "This whole time I was crying out for You to fill a room when what You wanted was to fill me." A deep grief came over my heart, at times, and thus repentance for looking past the personal connection the Lord was longing to have with me in the name of a corporate encounter. I could feel the grief and ache in God's heart because He was longing for me to know Him in fullness, but I had generalized it before I had personally experienced it. This grief and ache that I experienced was not a feeling of punishment, nor did it feel like a burden to bear. Instead, it was His closeness and availability that had been there all along that hit me at my core. In His closeness, I experienced His kindness leading me to repentance. I could feel that in my ignorance and lack of awareness I had unintentionally resisted

THE TEMPLE OF THE HOLY SPIRIT

the Holy Spirit when He was right there, ready to pour Himself out upon me. I didn't feel ashamed or guilty, but I did feel deeply convicted and moved that I must turn to Him and respond. I had now received something too precious, and to resist it would be to resist the Holy Spirit.

Because of the intimacy and closeness I felt with the Lord, and in the intensity of the power and fire that I was feeling, I could no longer escape that I had made some of the Gospel truth somewhat impersonal. What I always find challenging to explain is that I was not doing this intentionally, nor was I aware of this. Before this encounter, I would tell you that I loved Jesus deeply and that I was serving Him with the best that I had—and this was completely true. However, I believe that the fear of man operating in my life had become a hindrance, a dam of sorts that walled off some of the mighty flow the Holy Spirit was longing to pour out upon me, and He wanted to address it. He was coming after me, and all He needed was for me to lay down my self-constructed shield and allow Him to be my refuge.

When I look back through my journals and think back to myself pre-encounter, I see that the likely reason why I was asking God to fill a room instead filling me was because it felt easier to believe that He would fill a room because it had far fewer flaws than I did. Believing this magnificent King of Glory would want all of me, just as I am, was too much for my mind to comprehend. I used to think that when I became a leader or someone God would use in a mighty way, I would have it all together, or at least mostly together. I thought I'd feel confident in myself and have most of the answers. If I am honest with myself, I think I was hoping that I would be different, and not so human.

THE HOLY SPIRIT MADE HIS HOME IN YOU

But the Lord didn't set up the temple for His mighty Spirit in a room; He put His Spirit in a temple of flesh, in you! God's desire all along has been for a deep and meaningful connection with His children. We are His workmanship (see Ephesians 2:10), made for His pleasure, created for Him, by Him, and through Him. And not only are we fulfilled by Him, but He takes great delight in us. God could choose any place to be His dwelling place. He didn't have to call us His temple, but He is a relational God and He desired for us to be His home. That truth right there is enough to have me undone before Him for all my days. The King of Glory, the Alpha and Omega, the mighty God of all creation chose to dwell in man because He loves us and made us for communion with Him.

One of the most perplexing passages in the Bible to me is one I mentioned in the previous chapter. Paul in 2 Corinthians 12 talks about God's power being perfected in our weakness. I am not sure how God's power could ever be more perfect—I am quite convinced that it is perfect as it stands on its own—but God saw fit to construct a throne for His power in our places of lack, of weakness. *The Passion Translation* comments on this Scripture that our weakness is a portal for His power.

Think about that for a moment. The perfect place for the manifestation of God's power is in the place you would like to hide away, cover over, or just ignore. I used to think that my "weak places" were areas where I need to hide or strive for perfection. I was embarrassed by my insecurity and would often try to cover it with silence or with my own strength. But God in His mercy designed our surrendered humanity to be a place for Him to move powerfully in. All He asks is for us to surrender our weaknesses to Him, to make them an altar for His fire to fall on.

This Scripture is not a place to excuse our failures, but what it does communicate to me is that God is looking for a place to dwell that won't resist Him. He is looking for a place where we humbly submit ourselves to Him and invite His Spirit to come in and do a mighty work of transformation. When God comes into a circumstance, everything changes. Things that rob us die, and He resurrects His nature in its place producing the fruit that could only be born of His Spirit. When God fills our weak places, His power becomes evident, not just to us but to those around us.

This is the mystery revealed to the Gentiles that Colossians 1:17 talks about—that Christ dwells in us as His disciples, and His nature and heart being manifest in our lives is what gives hope to the world around us. There are many facets to this mystery, but one reason it is a mystery is that it is challenging to comprehend that Christ's glory would be revealed in earthen vessels. Without the sacrifice of Jesus, on our very best days and in our own strength we are not nearly pure or holy enough to be the house of God. But man didn't write this story; God did. Religion constructed by man's mind makes sense to man, but a story written by the King of Glory certainly is one of great and beautiful mysteries, far too merciful and beautiful for us to fully comprehend. This truth must be grasped in spirit.

The thought that God would call us and then empower us with His very own Spirit and reveal Himself through us is too great to fathom. God doesn't simply empower us with tools or constructs but empowers us with Himself. Through union and communion with the Holy Spirit, we walk in the fullness of the high calling of Jesus. It is in intimacy with Him that He prepares us to walk in our glorious inheritance. What is this inheritance, you ask?

Incomparably great power for us who believe
(Ephesians 1:19 NIV).

I was crying out for God to fill a room because I was able to comprehend the Lord wanting to love on people and touch their lives, but I had tried to keep this truth more impersonal to bypass a mystery I could not fully comprehend—I was His house, His chosen place to rest. Jesus Christ, the Son of God, the spotless Lamb, laid down His life willingly so that we might become His place of resting. He was crucified as a criminal so that our punishment could be bought once and for all so that we could enter into the fullness of relationship with God Himself. This is a message for us all.

JESUS GAVE US ALL AUTHORITY

Jesus stepped in, through His perfect sacrifice took back what the first Adam squandered, and now in Matthew 28 He returns. Three days after His death, He carries keys of authority (that He has taken from the serpent) in His hands and stands before His disciples ready to empower them to spread the Gospel message far and wide. I tell you what, if I were writing this story, I would likely have done it very differently. I may have told the disciples that they messed it up, humans are just fickle, and they missed it completely, and I would have gone to be with the Father, keys in hand to hatch up a new plan. But not our King, not our beautiful Messiah. In Matthew 28:18-19 (NIV), He hands the keys of authority back to what we consider mere men and says, *"All authority in heaven and on earth has been given to me. Therefore go and make disciples of all nations..."* after they are instructed to go wait in the upper room for the fulfillment of the prophecy in Joel 2. God wanted to pour out His Spirit on all flesh.

Before the outpouring of the Spirit in Acts 2, the Holy Spirit had rested on a place or a specific person who had an assignment from God. The Spirit of God would clothe a prophet, priest, leader, or king and would empower them to do the assignment God had called them to. You even see in Exodus 11 when Moses is finding the weight of his assignment too heavy to bear and so God takes a portion of the Spirit that was on Moses and distributes it among 70 priests so that they can help carry the weight that Moses had. Prior to this distribution, these 70 priests did not have the Spirit of God resting on them in that way.

The people of God in the Old Covenant would know God was with them, often through physical signs like the cloud by day and the pillar of fire in Exodus 13. Or when we see God instructing Moses to build the Ark of the Covenant (see Exodus 25) so His presence would dwell with His people. God so longed to be with them in their midst, and understood their need for Him that He had them construct something so that He could be in their midst. After Jesus went to the cross we came under the new covenant, the covenant of grace. The cross restored us back to original purpose—to walk with God and live in full connection with Him. Jesus made a way where there was no way, and now by His design we become the very tabernacle of the Holy Spirit, the place of His dwelling.

This was God's intent the whole time. Jesus came to destroy the works of the enemy, and in this season while we await His final return we are charged to walk as the prophetic sign and wonder of what is to come—Heaven on Earth. Joel 2:28-29 says that in the last days (the days we are living in) He will pour out His Spirit on all flesh. This is not some flesh or even most flesh but the desire of His heart is to pour Himself out lavishly on all. We know not all will receive this, but it is available to all those who surrender their lives to Jesus. The believer's life filled with the Spirit of God and lived displaying His glory is a signpost that God's Kingdom is at hand and is coming. The Spirit dwelling within us is the promise that we have a King who is alive within us and He has a Kingdom that belongs to Him and thus to those who receive Him.

AUTHORITY AND THE POWER OF THE SPIRIT

All of this theology is incredibly powerful and profound, but if it does not become real to us then it will remain simply knowledge. The way we are awakened to the great power and reality of Christ's work is by the wonderful work of His Spirit in us. The Spirit of God is our great awakening and necessary for every part of the Christian life and call. There is nothing of eternal significance we can do without Him. Once Jesus was resurrected from the dead, He met with His disciples and He breathed on them to receive the Holy Spirit in order to commission them to carry the Gospel of salvation for the forgiveness of our sins (see John 20:22). I believe we as the Bride of Jesus have become dull in understanding the Person of the Holy Spirit and His work in us, the people of God. We have clung to tradition and understood through a lens of opinions the work of the Holy Spirit but have become asleep to the biblical truth of who He is and His great work and power within us. The grasp of even a fraction of the revelation that we are the temple of God would drastically change our lives and how we live forever. The Spirit is not a thing or an "it"—He is the third Person of the Trinity and God Himself. The Person of the Holy Spirit is the honored guest and the treasured gift of the people of God, and this should not be taken for granted. We are not entitled to the Spirit, nor are we entitled to His operation in our lives. He is the gift Jesus gave to us, and He must not be grieved or quenched. The Holy Spirit is sensitive to our invitation and longing, and He deserves our honor, respect, and our worship. The honor of the Holy Spirit could never detract from Jesus because it is His role to glorify the Son and to bring to remembrance everything Jesus has said. The Father is not afraid of us seeking a relationship with the Holy Spirit for He is the Spirit of God and speaks not on His own (see John 16:13).

One of the things I believe is the greatest grievance to the Lord is the church's approach toward the Holy Spirit. Some believe that He is no longer in operation, while others treat Him like He's scary or some kind of ghost. I have not often seen the Holy Spirit push His way through a meeting or force Himself into a room. Of course, He is always there and present, but how often do we see Him made manifest? And when we reduce the Christian life to that—a form—we live a life of tradition with no power. The Holy Spirit is the power of the Godhead. He is the breath on the dry bones in Ezekiel 37. He is the very Spirit who raised Christ from the dead, and He is available to dwell in every believer.

We have spent many hours debating and asking questions about the Holy Spirit, but something I don't feel like we ask enough is, "What would my life look like if I accessed the fullness of what God has made available to me?" The Holy Spirit isn't an extra, nor is He an option in the Christian life; He is crucial to us living in oneness with Jesus, walking out our salvation, stepping into the Great Commission, and knowing the ways of our Lord. A life lived without dependence and surrender to the Holy Spirit is one full of striving, lacking power, and incredibly dull.

THE SPIRIT WORKS WITHIN US

It is only by the mercy of God that we receive His Holy Spirit, and He should be received as a treasured friend and as our Lord. To cooperate with the Holy Spirit is one of the greatest invitations that we get as Christians. The Holy Spirit is not looking for us to step aside so that He can move, but instead is looking for an invitation from us so that He can be made manifest in and through our lives to advance the Holy Kingdom of God.

When the Spirit of God moves in a room or a person, that moment is holy and not to be taken for granted. If we look at a spiritual moment by the flesh, we will not understand its power nor its significance. The flesh wants understanding and to know the purpose immediately, but when we walk in the spirit by faith, we realize God is doing a deep work, to be protected and valued till He brings it to completion. A life honoring the Holy Spirit and His work is one that clings to God Himself and every word that proceeds from His mouth. It is one that is willing to live in mystery and often with misunderstanding surrounding it for seasons at a time. We cannot explain everything the Lord does in each moment. Some gifts are too grand to comprehend; they must simply be received by faith and with humility.

We are in deep need of good teaching and true demonstration of how to cooperate with the Holy Spirit. Too often we miss the subtle move of the Holy Spirit in a room because we aren't taught how to live sensitive to His movement. The Spirit was made manifest as a dove (see Matthew 3); another time God's voice was not the earthquake but in the whisper (see 1 Kings 19:12). That tells me that He can come quietly looking for those who are hungry enough to look for Him. In order for what God is doing around us to take root in us, we must become aware of the move of the Spirit of God amongst us. When a moment takes place in the manifest presence of God, it has the capability to change and transform us forever when received properly. I believe there are times when we have come to treat the Holy Spirit as commonplace and therefore become too casual with the move of the Spirit; at times, we are even entitled toward Him. I don't think that this is anybody's heart, but in the abundance of His outpouring, this is when we must be vigilant to not squander the preciousness of what it means to be His temple.

In the 1990s, the Church experienced revival—the Holy Spirit awakened His people to His power and availability. Thousands of hungry or burned out missionaries, pastors, teachers, and believers gathered in different regions where a revival of the Church was taking place. They stood under the waterfall of the outpouring of the Spirit and were refreshed and filled up by His love. This is what happens when the Holy Spirit enters a room in a way that is beyond our ability. When the Holy Spirit comes and ignites revival, people are awakened to His power and the gifts of the Spirit start flowing with incredible ease (see 1 Corinthians 12). The Church has enjoyed the fruit of these mighty outpourings. Our worship, our teachings, and many gatherings following this have been marked by what the Holy Spirit has done during this time. For the last 30 years, many have been stewarding this outpouring of the Spirit and what it deposited in believers. We have seen the Church equipped with tools to operate healthily in the gifts of the Spirit, and in the last 20 years many schools have emerged, training people in His ways and wondrous works. Though this has been wonderful and according to His leading, I find myself recognizing this was just the start for our generation. He has more for us, and we need to be hungry for it.

I have been sensing that there is a familiarity the Lord is wanting to break off the body around the move of the Spirit. We have become knowledgeable and have grown accustomed to phrases. What once was first-love response is now a tradition we uphold. Familiarity is not always bad—it can be a sign that we know someone—but when familiarity causes us to not expect more beauty from them, to not pursue the new thing with them, familiarity becomes apathy. When we experience something so powerful and extravagant, we can run the risk of becoming familiar and satisfied, but the humble and hungry heart will long for more. We stay hungry by staying connected to Him. We must resist the temptation to find safety and power in what we know or have learned and instead find safety in our connection with Him—the infinite one.

I have seen in my own life, the more I experience the Lord, read His Word, and walk with Jesus, the more I come to know. Because of my growth in knowledge of the Lord, when the Holy Spirit starts moving in power in rooms I am leading or teaching in, I can feel this temptation to lean on what I know or understand. Sometimes it's a temptation to teach a principle, sing a familiar song, or start activating the gifts of the Spirit out of pressure to "do something." In the presence of God, nothing is impossible, and the excitement of possibility can take over. But these are the times to respond not react. It is in the softness of my heart toward Him that I truly move and operate with Him—where I let my knowledge of His ways become an invitation to go deeper with the Holy Spirit rather than stay in the shallows of what I have already discovered.

Our knowledge of the Lord must not become a construct we use to protect ourselves from dependence. It also can be a wonderful gift when carried with a deep sensitivity and desire for the Holy Spirit. Knowledge from the Lord with full dependence on Him will equip us to walk empowered by Spirit. It is in this place that we will do and see things we could not have dreamed. But knowledge without softness of heart puffs up and separates us from Him and each other. Operating in dependence on the Holy Spirit may not always result in what I expected to happen but no matter what, I am certain to learn something about Him. In my best attempt to follow Him I may end up singing the familiar song, or I may do something completely new but in it all my desire is to trust and not to default to leaning on my understanding. The Holy Spirit is not looking for perfection but for a heart that seeks to know Him and is willing to risk to go deeper into His heart.

I travel around the world speaking and teaching, and one thing I am acutely aware of is that the people of God are hungry for more and we have only scratched the surface of what is available in the person of the Holy Spirit. He is wanting to awaken us to an "Acts Church" again—dependent on Him and full of His fire.

HOSTING THE HOLY SPIRIT

I truly believe that there is a fundamental difference between us having the Holy Spirit and hosting the Holy Spirit. Being in covenant and being in love can be one and the same or fundamentally different. I have been married to my husband for 13 years now, and often in my day-to-day life I find myself busy carrying a lot on my mind, knowing I have a lot to get done. There are days when I arrive home from work and am greeted by my husband with a big smile and a hug while he asks me how I am. Many times, I'll give a quick answer and go straight to the kitchen to start preparing dinner and getting all the details covered for the household and our three young children. You can imagine our little home, full of buzzing minds and busy feet. Around 8 PM, everything starts to settle and our children are in bed. This is our time to connect or watch a show to unwind from the full day. Now if, while sitting on the couch, I take out my computer and begin to answer the emails that I didn't get to in the day, working on a project that didn't quite get tied up, what am I receiving from my husband? Though my husband is present, sitting right beside me, with my attention elsewhere I will never feel the benefit of the availability of my husband even though his love is right there.

It's only when I lay aside all that is trying to get my attention and allow myself to connect to the love that is there, to the presence that is available, that I truly reap the benefit of our connection.

Though our covenant is strong, I must not take for granted what is available to me.

At times we mistake covenant for connection. We make promises on our wedding day, and years down the line we may still be living true to many of them, but that does not mean we are experiencing deep connection and fruitful intimacy. Being true to my promise of not giving my heart to another does not always mean that I am living fully given to my spouse. The greatest benefit of our covenant is that covenant provides the safety to give each other the fullness of our presence. I can raise our children with my husband, Ryan, wash his clothes, and even sleep in the same bed, but if we don't make the effort to have meaningful connection and take time to be present to each other's presence, eventually our covenant will be that of a promise but will lack substance (power) and real living fruit.

This is where I believe many in the "Church" are—where the Bride of Christ is finding herself. She has made a promise to the Lord, and she may be living it out in the fundamentals of the covenant. But is she present in His presence? Is she alive to His availability? Is she experiencing the fullness of union and communion with Him as His dwelling place? An even greater concern that I have at times is that we have traded covenant and intimacy for an outcome. We have begun to treat the Holy Spirit like a tool, something we can use or utilize to get further in what we're made for or called to. Is Jesus becoming a stepping stone for our platform and our destiny? Or perhaps an addition to our story?

To treasure the Holy Spirit is to treasure the presence of God. This means that when we treasure the truth and manifestation of His presence with us, we treasure Jesus and the Father. God is not separate; He is one.

I feel very strongly about this as I believe we have under-estimated our need for God in our lives. In the face of great abundance in the world, we can begin to believe that we have all that we need. We forget that mercy was the thing that got us to where we are. When we do not recognize the lavish gift of mercy and grace, we begin to squander the tenderness of His presence with us. But the life given daily to Him, remembering the precious truth that God dwells within us, is the life lived sensitive to the moving of the Spirit.

I have a holy fear in my own life as I give myself to Him as a living sacrifice. When God begins to move unhindered in our lives, it is powerful and recognizable. It often comes with favor we do not and will never deserve, and He does not apologize for that. God designed us to reveal His glory, but we could never do it without His great mercy, which we need every day. In the Lord, there is a beautiful confidence we get to walk in, but there is also a holy reverence that must be at the forefront of cooper-ating with Him. I never want to forget my need for Him as I try to move in and with His glorious presence. God in His mercy chose people to collaborate with Him in order for His glory to be made known. It was His design. I wrestled with this for a long time before I ever began writing this book. Inside of me is a holy tremble because God has done something in me that only He could do and I have very little to do with it. I would never want to take something He gave me as a gift and utilize it for gain, and yet there is still a responsibility we all have to steward and increase what He has deposited.

God, however, has no tremble or fear in our role, because He is not afraid to partner with us, nor does He withhold from us. In fact, it's what He longs to do. He wants to partner up with you, and He has no problem with your person being attached to His story. Though the Spirit dwells within us we must not mistake that He is small enough to be contained by our frame. The Holy Spirit is not an additive to our destiny, He is not an addition to our call, He is everything that we need and is the power to make all the impossibilities possible.

I think many people think that there is a final destination we need to reach in order to be all that we are called to be. The "destination" of our lives is not something we do but who we become. Every day, the life yielded to the Spirit of God is one that is being formed into the likeness of Christ. A life that is lived in this way is fuller and more abundant than we know, and the adventures you get to be a part of are beautiful and exciting. When we focus on Jesus, living in His righteousness and pursing His Kingdom, all things are added.

LAYING ASIDE EVERY OTHER STRONGHOLD

The Spirit has not only purposed to live and dwell within us but His work in our lives enables us to live in the stronghold of the Lord. To remain in Jesus (see John 15:4) is to firstly forsake all other protective mechanisms we have constructed throughout our journey thus far. The challenge is that we find safety in strongholds, even bad ones. It's called a stronghold because that is what it is—a fortress. The fortress of the name of the Lord keeps us safe from the enemy (see Proverbs 18:10), but the stronghold of the enemy keeps us limited and bound. I remember a leader once saying that people will gravitate toward bad love if they believe they will have no love. That is something I have pondered many times. When we find safety in the fear of man or fear of rejection, it is because we believe that with the protection that stronghold will give us, though it's painful and limiting, at least we won't be completely exposed. When we live under the influence of the lie that God won't protect us or God won't come through for us—we begin to grab hold of a need to take care of ourselves instead of entrusting our lives to God. It is in repentance for believing these lies that we allow the truth to come in. The Bible actually promises that in this world we will have troubles, but Jesus follows on after that with, "But take heart, for I have overcome the world" (see John 16:33). It is not in the absence of pain that we find strength, but it is in knowing that God is with us, He has given us His very own Spirit to comfort and walk with us, and He promises that He will never leave you no matter how challenging it is. Not only is He with us, but He has already overcome that which seeks to destroy us. It is in Him we find our victory.

When we repent of finding safety in places other than Jesus, we come into alignment with His prevailing truth, and the lies we believe are replaced with the reality of His nature. He is Emmanuel, God with us; He never leaves us nor forsakes us; and He is not just God in the victory but He is God in the battle (see Psalm 24), present in every challenge we face. Laying aside these strongholds, we step into the fortress of His name (see Proverbs 18:10). In that place, we are safe and assured that He will finish what He has started in us (see Philippians 1:6).

CHAPTER 6

STEWARDSHIP OF THE GIFT

s we talked in the previous chapter, repentance is the exchange of the lies we are believing for the victorious truth of His nature. Exchanging our thoughts for His goes further than just replacing lies—it invites us to partner with Him in everything we do. Everything God created He designed to increase (grow) and be fruitful, and so long as the system is not broken and no limits have been placed on them, they will expand. The work of the Holy Spirit in us expands our capacity to receive, carry and reveal God's great Kingdom. This work takes our understanding beyond just knowledge in our minds or intellect, and enables our whole being (mind, will and emotions) to engage with God. God wants to advance His Kingdom in and through our lives through partnership and us cooperating with Him. I want to highlight two main ways that we can cooperate with the Holy Spirit. One way is when we steward the gifts that God has given us for His glory and to build His Kingdom. Many times we will do things in faithfulness and obedience because God has asked, but not necessarily because we strongly feel His presence prompting us. This can be your daily devotion, how you treat your family, loving your neighbor, and so many more things. Though it does not always feel as powerful, it is vital.

I think we often underestimate the natural gift because we don't feel like it is as spiritual, but the life of the believer is spiritual in every way. We are the living sacrifice unto the Lord. The stewardship of our gifts is important because our gifts are given by God and He values what He has given us. Not only do we have gifts, but our whole being is a gift to us from the Lord to steward. Our gifts are not just the tools we have but also our personality, passions, and drives. There is not one part of you that you designed and you alone have the ability to manage and control your attitude and beliefs. God has uniquely made you for a purpose, and He despises none of you. He loves your personhood because it is His chosen place of dwelling.

When we steward ourselves and the gifts that He has given us toward His glory and His Kingdom, we learn how to properly walk in His authority that He has given to those who believe. This authority we receive from the Lord is like keys to open and unlock His Kingdom in the realms of society we are part of. We see this in the story of the parable of the talents in Matthew 25:14-30. Many of us have heard this story preached. Jesus illustrates increase and authority connected to the stewardship of what has been given to us. The parable starts out with a wealthy man going on a journey, and he entrusts some of his servants with the wealth he has acquired. One he gives fives bags of gold, another two bags, and another one, and the Word says he gives according to their ability. The story goes on to tell us that the man who was given five bags and the other who was given two each doubled the amount that was given to them, but the one who had received one hid his bag in the ground.

After a long time the master of those servants returned and settled accounts with them. The man who had received five bags of gold brought the other five. "Master," he said, "you entrusted me with five bags of gold. See, I have gained five more."

His master replied, "Well done, good and faithful servant! You have been faithful with a few things; I will put you in charge of many things. Come and share your master's happiness!"

The man with two bags of gold also came. "Master," he said, "you entrusted me with two bags of gold; see, I have gained two more."

His master replied, "Well done, good and faithful servant! You have been faithful with a few things; I will put you in charge of many things. Come and share your master's happiness!"

Then the man who had received one bag of gold came. "Master," he said, "I knew that you are a hard man, harvesting where you have not sown and gathering where you have not scattered seed. So I was afraid and went out and hid your gold in the ground. See, here is what belongs to you"

(Matthew 25:19-25 NIV).

FAITH AND THE LENSES WE HAVE

In this parable, Jesus is illustrating how to steward gifts given to us. The first thing I recognize when reading this passage is that it requires faith to steward what we have been given. We have only been given one life, one body, one personality, and a limited number of days to walk out our God-given journey, and it is going to require faith in God and who He is in me to accomplish that. The first two men increased what they had been given by utilizing what they had for the benefit of the master. They stepped out and took risks, and the master was pleased. The third servant did the opposite. He took no risk, displayed little to no faith, and thus chose self-protection. We see him describe why he chose self-protection, and it was how he understood who was ruling him that determined the risk he took. I think somewhere in this servant's heart, how he perceived his master was lensed by how he saw himself. The other two servants did not have the same issue with the master, but he did. It's wonderful to be those two, but I have found in myself this servant who buried what he was given.

I distinctly remember receiving a word from one of our senior leaders here at Bethel, Kris Vallotton, in my early years on staff. I was young and with no level of prominent leadership in our environment but serving as best as I could where I had been entrusted with responsibility. It was and is truly one of the greatest privileges to be given influence at any level in an environment I had sacrificed everything to be a part of as a student. I was part of the leadership team of one of our student-attended services at our secondary campus here in Redding. I had been asked to take up the offering, and once I was done and was walking back to my seat, Kris stepped forward and said something so incredibly profound to me. He told me that I had a gift of communication and storytelling on my life. He went on to say that I needed to steward 30 minutes a day reading the Word and writing down everything the Lord showed me. I really liked what he was saying and felt very good about myself at that moment. But then he went on to say something that was profound. He said, "I need you to do this. I mean it." From there, he prophesied some significant things about my future here in Redding and within the Bethel environment. What he said to me felt too big for me to grasp. Don't get me wrong—it felt significant and powerful and something that I would have felt so honored to be a part of, but it hit a part of my heart that was lensed. I received the word with great joy; I felt valuable and strong in the moment; I was encouraged; but when I went to do what he had prophesied for me to do, I quickly lost motivation. My view of who I was and what I was not and how I believed God (my master) would approach the lack I felt was affecting the way that I stewarded this word.

When we don't know the nature of God and His desire to partner with us, when we don't know the goodness of God and His faithfulness toward us, we live restrained in His purposes. This fear the servant had was not the "fear of the Lord" but the fear of punishment. God disciplines and doesn't punish. Jesus bore our punishment on the cross to purchase our peace (see Isaiah 53:5). Discipline addresses the internal issues going on that are causing bad fruit, while punishment only address the external fruit. Discipline is with care for the person in mind and their health; punishment cares about how they appear and make the punisher appear. We never discipline our children so that we can look good; we discipline them for their sake to walk upright and strong in freedom, to lead them in the ways of the Lord and His grace.

THE FEAR OF THE LORD

I want to talk briefly about the fear of the Lord because it is vital for us to walk in healthy stewardship of the presence of God. When we reject the fear of the Lord because we liken it to unholy fear, we build a house without a needed part of its foundation, and we all know that house cannot stand. Proverbs speaks about the fear of the Lord many times. In Proverbs 9:10 (NIV) it says that *"the fear of the Lord is the beginning of wisdom."* This means that the foundation of wisdom is the fear of the Lord—it is the starting point that we build our wisdom and understanding upon. How we see God is vital to knowing Him and walking in the wisdom and understanding we need to steward what He has given. All knowledge and understanding that is not built upon the proper view and knowledge of God will not stand through storms and challenges.

Isaiah 11 talks of what will happen when the Spirit of the Lord (the Holy Spirit) rests upon Jesus. One of the distinct expressions

STEWARDSHIP OF THE GIFT

of the Holy Spirit resting and operating in the life of Jesus is the spirit of the fear of the Lord, and it declares that Jesus will take delight in the fear of the Lord.

> *Then a shoot will spring from the stem of Jesse,*
> *and a Branch from his roots will bear fruit.*
> *The Spirit of the Lord will rest on Him,*
> *the spirit of wisdom and understanding,*
> *the spirit of counsel and strength,*
> *the spirit of knowledge and the fear of the Lord.*
> *And He will delight in the fear of the Lord,*
> *and He will not judge by what His eyes see,*
> *nor make decisions by what His ears hear*
> (Isaiah 11:1-3 NASB).

The fear of the Lord is not to limit us but to liberate us. Fearing God is not the demonic fear we know but a holy fear and awe that brings us into alignment with Him as master. It is an awareness of His greatness and our smallness. He is not only merciful but He is also just; He is kind but He is also the Almighty and all powerful. His eyes that burn with fire are full of love and they are on us at all times—this must not escape us. The fear of the Lord keeps us aware of our absolute need for Him and it goes hand in hand with His nature of love and faithfulness. The fear of the Lord is awe and recognition of His absolute holiness and a great relief that we are in His covenant of grace. The tension between the two must be walked out in the believer's life because the emphasis on one over the other either creates crippling fear or absolute entitlement.

In our current world culture we are very happy to talk about love, but you preach holiness and it can feel like we are swearing. The Holy Spirit is the one who helps us walk in the fear of the Lord and His great love and mercy. He teaches us to hold the two hand in hand so that we might know God and serve Him in all of our ways. When we know God, we walk in holy understanding and can steward the wonderful gifts He gives us. Our gifts and the gifts of the Spirit must be stewarded in awe of and intimacy with the Lord—both necessary for health and increase in our gifts and His authority in our lives.

For us to experience an increase in our lives will require understanding and belief in who He says He is and trust in His Holy Spirit in us. To steward what He has given us well is to live in responsibility toward the Lord and in freedom to step out in faith, knowing He is with us and His Spirit is empowering us. To grow in authority in God is to steward well the resources He has entrusted to us. We should not and cannot compare what the other has because this passage clearly says each was given according to their ability. God has given you what you have the ability to steward, and as you do this you will be entrusted with more.

STEWARDING HIS GLORY

The other way that I want to highlight is cooperation with the tangible presence of God. This is the same as the reality of walking with God in the cool of the day in Genesis. Before sin entered the world, daily walking with God was meant to be our inheritance all along. The introduction of sin has caused a separation in our walk with Him, but the lavish and merciful gift of the cross and resurrection has restored us to this walk with Him. Now to do it.

A lot of people would call this cooperating with the tangible presence of the Holy Spirit or moving in the glory. The glory of God is the beauty of the very presence of God made manifest to people. There have been many individuals who have walked in a powerful expression of cooperation with the glory of God. In our circles, I often hear people talk about "the glory." I love that we do and have no problem with it unless we fail to recognize that the glory is not an object but a Person. Glory is the manifestation of the beauty of God's own Spirit, the Holy Spirit. Oh, that we would love when the beauty of the Holy Spirit starts moving through a room. Often this move of His glory is subtle and soft to start, personally or corporately. It requires sensitivity and humility to seek Him, to cooperate with such magnificence. I love worship, and I will worship in gratitude and faith for what He has done for me all my days. But there is something that happens when we worship with awareness of His presence—when we don't just sing about Him but we sing to Him. In this place, a laid down offering of love invites a resting of His presence in a way no one could will.

I can feel the question of what it feels like when the glory comes. The tangible movement of the Holy Spirit brings a quickening to our spirits. Natural time feels like it stands still and, in that place, we begin to experience the reality of the Kingdom and eternity. It seems like colors, sounds, thoughts, and our senses become sharper, crisper, and bright. Our faith begins to roar within us as we behold the glory of His presence and realize that eternity is our true reality. Great miracles happen easily in the atmosphere of God's presence and things that we have been longing for breakthrough in happen in a moment. There is a beauty that you can see or feel on a person or in a room where the Holy Spirit is making Himself known. It's something we can't quite describe because your spirit just knows it and senses it. There is a wonderful sharpness of mind and tenderness of heart that transpires when His glory fills a room. To "steward" what God is giving of Himself in these moments is really to give our full attention and affection to whatever He is doing. As we honor and adore His manifest presence, we are awakened to the wonder of Jesus and we enter into a keen awareness of our identity in Christ, our spiritual authority, and our inheritance in Him. The manifestation of His glory awakens us to the reality of the majesty of Jesus and the cross and allows us to move in great revelation of this because when He is known we also are knowing Jesus and the Father. When I talk about the Holy Spirit being known it is important to remember that He is not separate from the Father or the Son but all three are one.

Often in moments when the glory (the beauty of God) starts to manifest, we sense it subtly and can feel like we need to do something about it. Humans love to get results or know what the purpose of something is before we give ourselves to it. These can be great attributes for operating in the natural, to protect ourselves from being taken advantage of, but it does not serve us well in cooperating with the Holy Spirit. The sanctified mind yielded to the Spirit knows that when God's tangible presence is moving it is not time to get its hands "on the wheel" but time to simply obey and respond.

Our ability to recognize and respond to the subtle movements of the Holy Spirit most often determines the depth in which we will experience Him. I say most often because there are times when God waits for no one and just does as He pleases, and this is marvelous. Those sovereign moments are ones to enjoy, but the stewardship moments are when we must follow His ways. The Dove is looking for a peaceful place to rest, one that is not looking to try to manage Him (like we ever could) but to move as He moves and wait as He waits.

There are some usual ways we have experienced God move over the generations, and then there are, of course, the unusual, which tend to ruffle feathers. But we aren't in this because of what people think; we are in this because we want to know God. Some of the more typical ways I see the Holy Spirit's resting manifest is by people experiencing physical sensations on their body. For some they experience heat or cool sensations on their bodies. This could be feeling like a part of your body or your whole being is on fire, or a sweet refreshing presence like water flowing or wind blowing. We see the reference to the Holy Spirit like fire, wind, or water through the Word of God.

For some, when the power of God starts touching their bodies, they feel a sensation of electricity moving through them and they shake, others feel a weight on them that causes them to bow or in more extreme cases fall on the ground. We see through the Old and New Testament that often when the Spirit fell on them, they would prophesy and then in Acts 2 they of course spoke in tongues and they were perceived as drunk. I don't pretend to understand all these, but I certainly see references to God doing what He will throughout His Word. In Ezekiel 8:3 we see Ezekiel was picked up by his hair and taken into the atmosphere above the earth to be shown various things happening in Jerusalem. The Apostles being perceived as drunk in Acts 2 and Peter went into trances more than once (see Acts 10:9-23 and Acts 22:17-21). Other manifestations could be unusual things manifesting in front of our eyes. I was in the room a few times in 2012 when a cloud of gold dust swirled through the room in the Bethel sanctuary during a worship time we were in. I know there have been many who have critiqued this and called it fabricated, but that could not have been further from the truth. I watched a few times as this gold glitter dust would manifest, sometimes in more subtle ways, and the recognition of it did not detract from but magnified Jesus's presence with us. As we made space for what He was doing and Jesus was adored and valued, it increased.

The value of recognizing the manifestation is not to seek manifestation but honor the one who is taking delight in showing something of Himself and His Kingdom to us. God in our midst is to be treasured and recognized. We do not seek manifestation—that is foolish. We seek the presence of God and we honor it. I would not ignore and devalue a gift from my loved one; I cherish the gift they are giving me because I treasure the person deeply. The recognition of His resting is just the beginning of moving with His agenda. I am so grateful that we don't have to learn this in one moment, but we are granted a lifetime of moments to learn with Him and grow in our cooperation with the glory of God.

There have been moments when I have felt the Holy Spirit come to rest and I have moved too quickly or moved in the wrong direction. Not intentionally, of course, but in ignorance, and often in my own zeal. In our school of ministry, we are given incredible freedom as leaders to discern and move with what the Holy Spirit is doing. I have found myself in so many moments when I can discern the Spirit is moving, but I cannot always tell what the right response is. I have found myself in so many moments when I have preached and then prayed for an outpouring of the Spirit, the Holy Spirit starts moving and touching people and I find myself feeling clueless about what to do next. Do I wait? Do I pray? Do I share or sing?

I once sat down with Bill Johnson to ask him these questions, expecting him to have some sort of way or formula to solve my problem, but instead he began to ease my fear and encourage me that each moment was one to learn. Moments when I get to learn His nature, His ways, and what He loves. Instead of being fearful of getting it wrong, I now just do my best to cooperate with Him, and when I feel like I missed it I get to go back and find out where I moved left when He was going right, so the next time I can move with His leading.

We need to be willing to explore places with the Lord where we don't feel equipped or knowledgeable in how to lead it all. These help us discover the dance of partnership that we get to participate in with Him. I am not in this for me; I am in it to receive and host Him as my all in all.

OUR RESPONSE

It's vital for us to know the purpose of the Spirit's work in each of us so that we will know His value to us. Encounters are not just meant to touch us but to transform us and reveal God and His nature so we can represent Him to the world. This means that we must steward what we receive from Him by validating His work in us as well as through those around us. Validating His presence means that we give our time and attention to what we sense Him doing over anything else because, ultimately, we as people will protect what we value.

I remember the first car I drove here in Redding. It was a white 2002 Ford Focus, and at some point someone had completely dented the whole driver's side by accidentally accelerating into the parking space beside me instead of hitting the breaks. I often find myself rushing out of the door trying to make it to my meetings on time, and the way our driveway is set up, when I reverse from our carport there is always a long line of bushes running parallel to my car. In my hurried state, I would frequently find myself reversing so quickly that these bushes would scrape down my driver's side, but because this car wasn't very valuable to me I didn't think much of it.

A few years later, I had saved up for a car and bought my first ever brand-new vehicle. It was a 2013 Kia Soul, and I was so proud of it. My Kia Soul had no dents or scratches, and it had cost us many months of sacrifice to save up for this new car. The first time I reversed that car out of my carport, I drove slowly and kept adjusting to make sure I didn't drive it near those bushes. I realized that if I was going to protect my new car, I was going to have to adjust my morning routine so I could have the time to reverse carefully, because now I had something of value to me.

When we create value for things in our lives, we have to adjust to make room for those things, and this is no different with the Lord. When we come to value the presence of God and understand the power of His work in us and the body, we are faced with a need to adjust some of the things that we previously did. The only way we truly experience the fullness of what He is doing in us is by setting our agenda aside to worship Him and seek Him and make room for Him to move. When we fail to give attention and make the adjustments to the move of the Holy Spirit and His work, we can hinder the great work He is wanting to do in us. Of course, there is grace, and we all will miss it at times, but let us not let our human error become an excuse to stay stagnant and not lean in to adjust to His moving.

The work of the Holy Spirit in our lives is not to "fix" us but to use every circumstance to help form Jesus within us. God does not waste one moment in the lives of those who love Him. And those willing to surrender to the ways of the Spirit will see that He is working in us so that we start to love like Jesus, look like Him, think like Him, act like Him. Our lives reveal Jesus and His great Kingdom to a lost and dying world. There is no way that we ourselves can live like Jesus in our own strength, and God knows this. That is why it is the good pleasure of the Father to give the Holy Spirit to us, for it is He who does the great work of transforming us into Christ-likeness.

Take a moment and think about how Jesus is being formed in your life in this season. What facet of His character is He forming in you right now? The Holy Spirit is at work in your life and in the lives of people around you to make us like Jesus in every part of our lives so that we may be like Him. A life that looks like Jesus's life is the most fulfilling life we could live. God wastes nothing, and will use even our toughest circumstance for our good. Though He doesn't create hardship for us He will use it to strengthen our faith and build the hope of Christ in us (see Romans 8:28 and Romans 5:3-5). He has a purpose in us even when we are pressed on every side. What circumstance is challenging you? Ask the Holy Spirit how He is working in you to work it for your good, forming the nature of Jesus in you. During my encounter and after it, I have spent much time in the Bible learning about God's Spirit and receiving teaching from men and women in the faith who have stewarded these powerful encounters before.

It has taken me the last three years of stewardship to just begin to learn to cooperate with what He started and to learn of His ways from what He deposited in me. Three years of time with the Lord, processing and pondering what I experienced, three years of sharing my story in nearly every environment I have been invited to, and I am still learning about what God gave me in those six weeks. After sharing my story over a hundred times, the Holy Spirit will still prompt me to share it, and without fail He will come powerfully to meet His people every time. I myself still weep at different points of this story because of how life altering it was and is for me. At times I feel foolish sharing my story again, questioning if I look like I have nothing else to say or no depth, but I know it is only by cooperating with Him that true life is released to His people.

Many people have powerful encounters with the Lord, but it takes intention to continue leaning in to the intimacy they experienced in those moments. Many times, people have come to me feeling as though when the intensity of the encounter lifted they had failed or done something wrong. In reality, it was now time for them to discover and steward what they had received. It is not the manifestation of the encounter that is the true prize but the revelation of who God is and what He wants you to know of Him that we must treasure and grow in. This can only be done by giving our time, energy, and affection intentionally to Him and His Word. It is us taking our intentional "secret place" time with the Lord and allowing it to create a secret place within our hearts. When we become aware that we are the dwelling place of the Holy Spirit, we understand that we are to host Him. This is where we learn to cultivate a place where we can steward our heart toward the reality of God with us, every moment of every day. What a glorious gift we have been given.

Though God designed us to be filled with His Spirit as individuals, He also designed us to collectively be unified in the Spirit and to experience Him as the corporate body. In the last chapter, we talked about being the temple of the Holy Spirit. Paul is one of the major writers in the New Testament about us being the temple of the Holy Spirit. Whenever Paul speaks of the individual as a temple, he often contrasts with the corporate body being the temple as well. The intent of God was that we would learn to cooperate with Him as an individual and thus would learn to cooperate with Him together.

A lot of people will say that unity brings about revival, but in the book of Acts we see that it's actually the outpouring of the Spirit that brings forth a radical unity in the birth of the Church. Of course, unity has choice involved, but there is a greater unity that we can achieve, which goes beyond our own ability to choose one another. It's in the outpouring of the Spirit on a company of people that creates a bond that cannot be broken. It is not a unity of agreement but a unity of submission under one God, one head—Christ Jesus—and one Spirit that joins us together. Unity in the Holy Spirit creates honor in our hearts for others and their unique design. It leads to a great freedom for each of us as individuals to be who we were created to be, bringing our unique strengths to the benefit of the body. When we recognize that our neighbor is a temple of the Holy Spirit, we learn to value and recognize His gifts and work in them and will thus learn to cooperate with other expressions that differ from ours. Responding well and with humility to the Lord moving in our brothers and sisters is vital to cooperating with the Holy Spirit corporately.

THE GIFTS OF THE SPIRIT AND INTIMACY

I love the gifts of the Holy Spirit, and I love watching them in operation. I marvel at the mighty work of the Holy Spirit in the ordinary man or woman's life. It is the Lord's good pleasure and His desire that we would operate in these gifts, so the church may be strengthened and encouraged to build the Kingdom. The Lord has given us the Holy Spirit so that these gifts can come alive in us and be filled with His power so that we can manifest Heaven's reality on earth. This is part of the Ephesians 4:11-16 (NASB) mandate:

> And He gave some as apostles, some as prophets, some as evangelists, some as pastors and teachers, for the equipping of the saints for the work of ministry, for the building up of the body of Christ; until we all attain to the unity of the faith, and of the knowledge of the Son of God, to a mature man, to the measure of the stature which belongs to the fullness of Christ. As a result, we are no longer to be children, tossed here and there by waves and carried about by every wind of doctrine, by the trickery of people, by craftiness in deceitful

scheming; but speaking the truth in love, we are to grow up in all aspects into Him who is the head, that is, Christ, from whom the whole body, being fitted and held together by what every joint supplies, according to the proper working of each individual part, causes the growth of the body for the building up of itself in love.

Here we see that the fivefold ministry exists to equip the saints (people of God) to do the work of building up the body of Christ so that we might become mature, unified, and reach the fullness of Christ in us.

I feel that in this season of equipping the body to walk in the gifts of the Spirit we must ensure to keep the main reason that we have been given these gifts at the forefront of our teaching. The Holy Spirit is working in us in this season to bring to remembrance God's purpose in it all. There has been a mighty move in culture toward humanism, and I see it affecting the Church in many ways. Humanism puts us at the center of the story, causing life to revolve around us and how we perceive or experience things. I believe wholeheartedly that God wants us to live healthy and free lives in which we experience love and freedom, but that does not come through humanistic principles but by the ways of God at work in us. Freedom does not come from my perceptions or my experiences but from His truth living and permeating every part of my being. The Holy Spirit is the one who leads us into all truth and brings the transformation we need in order to be free. I feel concerned that we have become so content with our process and principles that we have, at times, forgotten the true power of the Spirit and His miracle working power in our lives and the lives of others. When I come to a problem with my tool first and consult God later, I have placed my knowledge over His leading. This can be subtle and easy to do, and we must adjust when we see that start to happen.

Tools are helpful, but they are best operated in accordance with the Inventor/Creator and His Manual. There is no more liberated life than the life that lives under the lordship of Jesus and serves His will, for His ways are not our ways—they are higher than ours, and He invites us to know His ways through His Word and His Spirit.

> But when he, the Spirit of truth, comes, he will guide you into all the truth. He will not speak on his own; he will speak only what he hears, and he will tell you what is yet to come. He will glorify me because it is from me that he will receive what he will make known to you. All that belongs to the Father is mine. That is why I said the Spirit will receive from me what he will make known to you (John 16:13-15 NIV).

Jesus is the ultimate goal—He is the prize, He is the way, and He is the destination. There is no higher destiny or gift that could be above the beauty and the freedom that Jesus is and brings. I'm sure we all know this in our minds, but I don't always see this in operation in the people of God. The awareness that Jesus can actually be more than sufficient for each of us, in every way and everything. We're not utilizing Jesus as a path for us to get to fullness—He is actually fullness itself. This is what the Holy Spirit does for us—He awakens us to the reality of Jesus, to His authority, power, and glory, and He works in our lives so that we would not just know this but would experience it in its fullness.

It has always been the intention of God that His presence would not just simply rest on an anointed man or woman but would rest on a people. It is powerful to see the Holy Spirit rest on one person's life. I've stood and marveled many times at men and women of God who have lived their lives in such a way with Holy Spirit that they operate in oneness with Him like a few do. But these lives are not meant to be a limitation for the body but an invitation for us. The life operating in the power of the Holy Spirit and carrying a manifestation of His glory is meant to provoke the everyday believer into a place of realizing that we could walk in this way too. The hope of the Lord is not simply that there would be a few individuals filled with His glory, but that we would be fitted together as living stones, as one tabernacle, to hold and host the glory of God and reveal that His Kingdom is at hand.

We are His body, which means we are to be His hands and feet, doing the work He started, with Christ as the head to reveal Him to the world. Jesus paid for us to walk in this, not just in form but endowed by His power. Jesus's life laid down on the cross is far too precious for us to simply pursue just one part. We must seek the fullness of His Kingdom and His righteousness.

The goal of the gifts of the Spirit—like prophecy, discerning spirits, gift of miracles—is that we would build one another up in the body so that we might walk in unity and become like Jesus. The reason why Paul exhorts us in 1 Corinthians 14 to earnestly desire the gift of prophecy is because it reveals the work and purpose of Jesus and what He is forming in a believer's life. Prophecy keeps our eyes on what Jesus is doing in our lives and how we can partner with Him. Take a moment to think about that. When we receive a word about running a business, feeding the poor, filling a stadium this is not about our greatness but about the fact that Jesus is initiating a supernatural work in our lives and we get to (and need to) partner with Him in it. The gift of prophecy initiates or reminds the people of God that God has a plan for their lives; He lives in them and serves as an encouragement to continue in the work that Jesus has set for them to do.

Our spiritual gifts are not just tools, they are mighty weapons that have the capacity, when yielded to the Spirit, to carry the most powerful presence the world has ever known.

> *The Spirit of God, who raised Jesus from the dead, lives in you. And just as God raised Christ Jesus from the dead, he will give life to your mortal bodies by this same Spirit living within you* (Romans 8:11 NLT).

The Holy Spirit is the greatest power the world has and will ever experience. He was there in the creation story breathing on the dust when Adam was formed. He was the breath in Ezekiel

37 when Ezekiel prophesied over the dry bones that became a mighty army, and He is the Spirit who raised Christ from the dead and seated Him high above every authority, ruler, and principality.

The angel of the Lord declares in Zechariah that it is *"'Not by might nor by power, but by my Spirit,' says the Lord Almighty"* (Zechariah 4:6 NIV).

This declaration is so incredibly powerful because already there have been many displays of great miracles in the people of God, and they are surely about to see an incredible display of the power of God in the time to come. This passage tells us that it wasn't through the might or the power of men that the miracles happened, but by the power of the Spirit of the Living God. One would think that this means God wants us to step back and just let Him do it all, but this is not the case. Though we can lose sight of the purpose of the gifts, though we could misuse them, God still desires that we would work together. To walk in the power of the Holy Spirit, it requires us to come to the table. Many people want to step out of the way and let God move sovereignly, but that is not what He desires. Of course, God can and does at times move sovereignly, but that is not how He ultimately wrote the story. He wrote us into His plan of redemption, and the solution was that He would give Himself to us fully and completely so that we could accomplish it together.

The gifts of God don't have to distract us from our ultimate purpose. A heart that walks in intimacy with God, endeavors to keep its eyes fixed on the one who empowers all things supernatural, and remembers that it is He who is doing a great work in them will stay the course. To bear lasting fruit in the Kingdom requires us to abide and remain fully connected to the Lord in our hearts and minds. This is the wonderful work of the Spirit in us. The promise of the Holy Spirit is the promise of cooperation and communion with God, and this life glories Jesus through the abundance of gifts given by Him.

Every gift, encounter, anointing, or grace is all to point to the King of kings and the vastness of His Kingdom. In a world preoccupied by our own agenda, the Church needs to become intimately acquainted with the beauty and victory of Jesus. Our God-given gifts operating from deep intimacy and dependance on the Spirit point to our generous and victorious King, full of mercy and all-powerful in every way.

> My prayer is that we as the body of Christ would be wealthy in His gifts and even more so hungry for His presence. I pray that we would be like Moses not willing to go anywhere Your presence does not go (Exodus 33:15). May we have a heart to know You, Lord, and thus a deep dependance on Your Spirit. May every mountain top or deep valley be a place where Jesus is glorified in our lives. God, would You sensitize us toward the moving of Your Spirit and makes us hungry to know You more in every opportunity. Teach us to host the Holy Spirit well and make room for Him to lead and move among us.

CHAPTER 7

ENCOUNTERS WITH
THE HOLY SPIRIT

I have the privilege of traveling around the world and visiting churches in different countries and getting to know many amazing people from different backgrounds. I spend a lot of my time in more charismatic environments but also visit more conservative churches. My second home growing up was the church. The Methodist church where my parents were on the pastoral leadership team has always been a place that has been more open to the move of the Holy Spirit than one would typically expect. Though we had little teaching around the move of the Spirit, there was always a hunger for freedom in the Lord. Many in the church had experienced "accidental moves of the Spirit," my parents being some of them. My mom and dad had led the youth group in their early 20's, and during this season they had experienced an unexpected outpouring of the Holy Spirit. Though they had no clue what to do, it gave them a hunger to seek for more. From a young age, I remember attending some more "charismatic" conferences that other churches were hosting. I grew up in the 90's when revival was rampant through the North American continent and spreading like wildfire, and it certainly spread all the way to our smaller coastal city in Port Elizabeth, South Africa.

These moments when the Spirit of God would come crashing into our meetings, homes, and lives gave us a taste of something we couldn't comprehend but created a deep hunger for a greater reality than the one we were experiencing.

REALITY OF THE SPIRIT REALM

Our existence here on earth matters far beyond our time here. The believer's mandate is to advance the Kingdom of God and establish the rule and reign of the Kingdom wherever we go. We don't do this by physical might or power but by the might and power of the Spirit of God.

Encountering the Holy Spirit goes beyond a personal experience. The personal experience of the Spirit awakens us to the reality of the power of God, His availability, and thus our authority in Him. When we encounter God, we become awake to the reality that we are not simply here on earth but there is a realm that goes beyond our comprehension and in fact that realm rules the natural realm.

> For we do not wrestle against flesh and blood, but against the rulers, against the authorities, against the cosmic powers over this present darkness, against the

spiritual forces of evil in the heavenly places (Ephesians 6:12 ESV).

And raised us up with Him, and seated us with Him in the heavenly places in Christ Jesus (Ephesians 2:6 NASB).

FAITH AND THE SPIRIT REALM

Faith is vital in the walk of the believer. Faith is belief in what we cannot see but know is real. Faith is the stake in the ground that holds to a Kingdom that is far greater than the kingdoms of this world. Faith is a "now" belief, a "now" hope. Faith is not a "someday" feeling but a deep assurance that what is in the Kingdom is mine because it has been purchased. Faith is like holding the keys to a car that may not be right in front of you but you know it is just around the corner, because just the day before you saw it. It's that "I just know it" feeling you get.

I want you to think about your beliefs in unseen things. We can be quick to judge a hopeful belief, but often slow to question a fearful belief. Faith and fear are both beliefs in the unseen. Faith is belief in an ever-advancing Kingdom of a good God who seeks to save, restore, and resurrect beauty and wholeness. Fear is an overinflated belief in the power of an enemy that wants to steal, kill, and destroy. Fear is a defense mechanism, and it comes from not being grounded in what Jesus has given us. It is a "just in case something goes wrong, I'll be ready" mindset.

It prepares us for the worst so that we will not feel exploited or disappointed. I don't want to diminish the fact that fear may shield us to some measure, but I also want you to know that fear severely limits us. It caps us off in every area of our life and numbs us to the benefits of true joy, hope, and freedom.

There have been so many moments in raising my children when we parents have had the choice between the fear message or standing on who God says He is. I will never forget a season we went through when our two oldest children, who were toddlers at the time, were having respiratory issues due to a wildfire here in Redding that nearly burned up our whole city. We had already been dealing with so many what felt like physical attacks on our family, and now our children's breathing was compromised. On and off for months we would wake up to our oldest struggling to breathe. We were constantly giving breathing treatments to each of our little ones day in and day out. Just when we were getting better and our children's health was drastically improving, we got hit again. I thought we had overcome what I believe was an attack from the enemy, and I am sure in measure we had, but this felt like his last-ditch effort to throw me off.

I had just preached at our Friday night service at Bethel on blind Bartimaeus crying out for Jesus to heal him. I had preached with conviction and passion about Jesus healing us and His heart to restore, and when I arrived home to kiss my kids while they were sleeping, I noticed our son's eye was a little swollen. I put a little ointment on it and didn't think much more about it till he woke me up a few hours later in the middle of the night to let me know his eye was really hurting. What was a slightly swollen eye was now getting quite large and concerning. We tried some remedies we had here at home for a few hours, but slowly his eye just got worse. We decided to take him into the urgent care but truly were expecting it to be something completely curable.

The doctor came in and examined him, and this was where it all changed for me. Our doctor began to talk of potential blindness and, if things continued, hospitalization and possible brain infection. The thought of my three-year-old losing his sight in one eye, let alone a brain infection, began to flood my being, and I felt completely overwhelmed. They gave him a couple of shots and sent us home with some medication, but if things didn't turn around in the next 12 to 18 hours, we were headed for the hospital.

I was trying to be strong but internally was a mess. When we arrived home, I called one of my closest friends and coworkers, Dave, and just shared my fear and thoughts. I was riddled with "what if," "why," and starting to believe that it was my pursuit of God that was harming my children. The enemy had got me so wound up and full of fear of him that I was ready to pull back in every area. Dave began to pray and as he did, he had a vision of Heaven's report of my son. Dave began to tell me about his vision and how God's report said he was going to be fine. As I listened, I knew he was speaking the truth, but it felt scary to embrace it because what if he was wrong. In that moment I chose to believe what I felt the word of the Lord was over the word of fear. That night my husband and I sat in our son's room while he slept and took communion and prayed what our friend had shared with us about Heaven's report over our son. We did all we could to anchor ourselves in faith, though it did feel vulnerable to believe for the best. The next morning our son woke up and his eye had come down significantly. We were now able to see just a little of his eye through a tiny little slit. I immediately asked him to cover the good eye to see if he still had sight, and to my great joy he could see.

Faith is a vulnerable, arms-wide-open stance that ventures into the unknown and grabs hold of impossibilities with belief that something is about to happen. Faith clings to an eternal reality that says at the end of all this, we win. And from that place of the victory of Jesus, I walk in full confidence that either right now or very soon I will see the goodness of the Lord. Faith is not for the faint of heart; it's the grueling wrestle with God, and you may walk away from it with a limp (see Genesis 32:24-32). But you will meet Him face to face and carry a ferocious conviction that He is with you. The conviction that God is with us is the most powerful and beautifully terrifying truth a believer could have. It's beautiful because it speaks of Heaven's reality and terrifying because we feel little control in it all. When we go from belief in Him with us to living in the conviction of this, no circumstance could shroud the flaming fire of perseverance in that man or woman, but the journey can be challenging.

Encounters are a vital part of the believer's life because they take our belief from head knowledge to experiential conviction. When our friend Dave encountered God's reality, we came alive to the reality of Heaven and our faith in our victorious Jesus was awakened. The Holy Spirit is the seal of our faith (salvation) (see 2 Corinthians 1:22), the deposit we receive as evidence that we have received an unshakable Kingdom in Jesus. He also is the giver of the gift of faith, and any time we feel shaky in our belief in God's promises we can ask the Spirit for help and for Him to strengthen us to stand in the fight of faith. Faith in God awakens our senses to the realm of the Kingdom, and in turn we see, hear, and know more about it and we confidently hunger for more. We were born to experience God with our whole selves—body, soul, and spirit. As we hunger for more, we receive more, and as we receive more, we grow in confidence in Him. The journey of faith has shaking involved in it. Do not be dismayed when you find yourself shaken within, for He is establishing a Kingdom that does not move when everything around you does.

> And His voice shook the earth then, but now He has promised, saying, "Yet once more I will shake not only the earth, but also the heaven." This expression, "Yet once more," denotes the removing of those things which can be shaken, as of created things, so that those things which cannot be shaken may remain. Therefore, since we receive a kingdom which cannot be shaken, let's show gratitude, by which we may offer to God an acceptable service with reverence and awe; for our God is a consuming fire (Hebrews 12:26-29 NASB).

FAITH AWAKENS OUR SPIRITUAL SENSES

When my son, Aiden, was around six years old, he started coming to my bed every night and wanting to sleep with us. Aiden is incredibly perceptive and is sensitive to those around him and the spiritual atmosphere. This sensitivity is a God-given gift that he has. I call this a "knower" or "feeler" gift; he perhaps doesn't see things in the spirit or hear things but he perceives them in his mind and heart.

It was during the pandemic that he started to appear next to my bed every night. The world was in turmoil and we all were facing fear (which is a spirit) at a level the world collectively had not faced for a long time. After a few nights of my son showing up at my bedside in the middle of the night, I sat down with him to see if I could figure out what was going on. He had already told me that he had not had any bad dreams but was just simply afraid.

It was on the way to school that I began to ask why he was feeling so scared and if anything had happened that would have caused this. As most six-year-old boys would respond, he shrugged it off and told me that he didn't know. We talked about commanding fear to go in Jesus's name and the authority we have in Him. I pressed in a little more and asked if we could say a short prayer asking the Lord to show us how the fear got in. He agreed and we did.

The next morning while driving to school Aiden randomly blurted out, while in conversation about things totally unrelated,

"Mom, I saw feet." I was perplexed by this statement at first, but something in my spirit knew that he was unveiling something important. I paused and asked him if the feet he saw were scary or good. He let me know that they were scary and he knew they were something spiritual. A little taken aback I jumped into warfare mode again, explaining spiritual authority, and we prayed and declared that all fear needed to go, etc. Though all of that is great to do, I knew I was missing something. My son had never seen in the spirit. We talked a lot about God speaking and practiced hearing God's voice, and thus far my son had never seen a picture or impression. I was bothered that my son, who has Jesus in his heart, was seeing demonic things in the spirit because our home belongs to the Lord. I began to ask the Lord, throughout my day, to give me a key to this. Why was my son all of a sudden seeing in the spirit but not seeing angels and all the good things? The Lord began to speak to my heart about fear.

The Holy Spirit told me that our senses are gates to the unseen and that fear and faith are what open the gates of our senses. He let me know that the fear the world around him was experiencing had affected my son and that it had opened his eyes. Then the Lord said to me, "Hayley, I want you to close the gate of fear over Aiden's eyes." I immediately wanted to do that but had no idea how. He said, "You close the gate of fear by opening the gate of faith in Me." This was the key I needed. It wasn't about speaking to fear, it was about my son encountering God and His Kingdom that would shift the fear he was experiencing.

That night we talked about the reality of the Kingdom of God and the power of the Holy Spirit, about how the name of Jesus is bigger and stronger than anything we could face. We talked about the angels and how they are sent by God to protect us from anything the enemy tried to throw our way. I knew God spoke loudly to Aiden's heart and felt led to invite the Holy Spirit to speak to him there and show us the reality that Jesus's Kingdom is with us now. We did a little activation together as we asked God to whisper to his heart where Jesus had sent angels to protect us in our home and what they were doing.

It took a little while, but all of a sudden, my son started to experience God speaking to him and showing him where God's angels were and how protected and covered he was. As Aiden started to experience this, his demeanor went from fearful to excited. He became more interested in the activity of Heaven in our home over the activity of the demonic. The truth of the greatness of God and His Kingdom overshadowed the ploy of the enemy. We prayed for Jesus to open his eyes to the reality of the Kingdom, and the very next day my son, who had never seen anything of the Kingdom of Heaven with his natural eyes, saw the angel of the Lord he had perceived the night before instead of the scary feet of the enemy. You can imagine what happened next. Aiden was no longer startling me at 3 a.m., standing over my bed in fear. He was now sleeping soundly through the night because he was assured that God was with him. This is the power of an encounter with God, and this is what the Holy Spirit can do for each of us. The Spirit of God will open our eyes to the greatness of Jesus and the power of His Kingdom and thus destroy the power of the work of the enemy in our hearts and minds.

Lift up your heads, you gates, and be lifted up,

you ancient doors,

that the King of glory may come in!

Who is the King of glory?

The Lord strong and mighty,

the Lord mighty in battle

(Psalm 24:7-8 NASB).

When we connect to the Lord in faith, we welcome the God of battle—our God who is strong and mighty. He overshadows every ploy of the enemy in our lives and reveals Himself as the strong one who sees all we are walking through. This mighty King of Glory cares to include Himself in our battles, big or small, and wants us to know He is mighty to save.

Another powerful passage about this subject is 2 Kings 6:15-19 (NASB):

Now when the attendant of the man of God had risen early and gone out, behold, an army with horses and chariots was circling the city. And his servant said to him, "This is hopeless, my master! What are we to do?" And he said, "Do not be afraid, for those who are with us are greater than those who are with them." Then Elisha prayed and said, "Lord, please, open his eyes so that he may see." And the Lord opened the servant's eyes, and he saw; and behold, the mountain was full of horses and chariots of fire all around Elisha. And when they came down to him, Elisha prayed to the Lord and said, "Please strike this people with blindness." So He struck them with blindness in accordance with the word of Elisha. Then Elisha said to them, "This is not the way, nor is this the city; follow me and I will bring you to the man whom you seek." And he brought them to Samaria.

I was profoundly impacted by this time with my son and was moved by the power of God to lead us as a family into such a special and real moment with the Lord. I began to wonder how many people in their childhood had seen things in the spirit and were told it was their imagination or had no one to talk to and just shut their senses down because of fear. The Holy Spirit began to talk frankly with me about how this moment with Aiden wasn't just for us but was a prophetic picture for His Bride. He was bothered by how many of His children were under attack by the spirit of fear, and He was making provision for it. He said to me, "Hayley, it is time that the prophets close the gate of fear over My people and open the gate of faith. My prophets are called to open the eyes of My people to the reality of My power and My Kingdom. Awaken My Bride to who I am."

There is an awakening for the Bride—it is the awakening to the reality of the God's eternal Kingdom.

LOVE AND FEAR

When we step into faith and begin to understand that we are living in a spiritual reality and not just a natural world, we become aware that our beliefs and words matter far more than what we see in the flesh. If by faith God spoke and the world was created, then our words too have spiritual power to either tear down the works of the enemy or build them up. What we believe in our heart flows from our mouth, and it is vital that we guard our hearts to live connected to faith in Him. There is too much backbiting, petty disagreement, and "canceling" among the people of God. When we become disconnected from the reality of the living God, we lose our faith in Him and His mighty power. In this we cling to tradition and form; we become puffed up with knowledge and lack the substance of love. Perfect love casts out fear, and we can only know perfect love if we know Jesus. The Spirit has come to us as the Spirit of adoption so that we might know the love of God, our Father, and carry great faith in it. It is when we put our faith in His great love for us that it begins to flow through our lives to others and it is by our love that the world will know we belong to Jesus.

I pray that out of his glorious riches he may strengthen you with power through his Spirit in your inner being, so that Christ may dwell in your hearts through faith. And I pray that you, being rooted and established in love, may have power, together with all the Lord's holy people, to grasp how wide and long and high and deep is the love of Christ, and to know this love that surpasses knowledge—that you may be filled to the measure of all the fullness of God (Ephesians 3:16-19 NIV).

True love as defined in 1 Corinthians 13 is supernatural. The world is trying to redefine love into a natural form that is so fluid and loosey-goosey. When love is not connected to the one who is Love, then it becomes confusing and fragile. Love becomes subjective when it isn't defined by the Subject. To truly embrace one another as Jesus embraces us, we have got to be fully reliant on the work of the Spirit of God to reveal and establish His love within us. The Holy Spirit, the Spirit of adoption, longs to baptize us in the love of God so that we might be rooted and established in the love of Christ. This rooting and establishing allows us to love like He does, and that enables us to know His great power altogether and not just as individuals.

THE HOLY SPIRIT AND THE WORD

As we have seen in this chapter, encounters awaken us to the reality of the spirit realm, to the victorious power of Christ and to His great love that conquers fear. Not only did I enter into these wonderful realities in God but I also fell in love with the Word of God. I am not sure that people always anticipate this to be a fruit of encounter with the Holy Spirit, but we should absolutely expect this. I think at times we have categorized people into groups of those who "have encounters and experiences with God" versus "people who like to study the Word." But during and following my encounter the Bible came alive to me in a way I had never experienced. Reading the Word is an encounter itself if we read it with a heart that seeks to know the Lord. I have always enjoyed the Bible, but something happened to me when I encountered the Lord. The Holy Spirit woke up a passion and unquenchable hunger for the living Word of God in a way I had not known. The Word of God became alive to me like God Himself was there stirring my heart with hunger and teaching me. This is because He was. An insatiable hunger came over me to seek after His Word because I had been introduced to the person of the Holy Spirit and I had a desperate desire to know Him more. I knew He was there, all over the pages, explaining God's nature and ways, His mysteries, opening heavenly realities, and showing me Jesus' heart and intention on every page. I became ravenous for the Word of God, and He met me there and has been ever since.

> "The Bible is the only book in the world where you read the book and the author shows up."
>
> **—Bill Johnson**

There is a huge threat facing the Church today. It is something that I believe has been creeping into our belief system around the Word of God and the invalidation of the authority of it. So many believers are questioning if God's Word carries "all authority" and if it is complete. When we take the Scriptures into question, we break our very foundation. The Bible is, of course, true and historically accurate, but it is more than just history; it is *"Spirit and life"* (John 6:63 NIV). The words of God in the creation story not only were a declaration or an announcement, but they carried the DNA and the power to create the moment they were uttered. The Word of God is not just true, it is the highest truth. It not only speaks it creates, tears down, builds, restores, establishes, fortifies, comforts, encourages, aligns, activates, demonstrates, and the list goes on. It has the ability to separate His words in us from the carnality within our own being and bring strongholds that have sought to rule us crashing to the ground. If you allow it, the Word of God will read you more than you read it, meaning it will expose and separate things in us if we yield to it.

> For the word of God is alive and active. Sharper than any double-edged sword, it penetrates even to dividing soul and spirit, joints and marrow; it judges the thoughts and attitudes of the heart (Hebrews 4:12 NIV).

The Word is an invitation to encounter God. When our heart is warm to the presence of the Holy Spirit as we sit down to read the Word, we enter into a powerful encounter with the living God and His nature. Our Bible is a constant invitation to know Him. Grieving the Holy Spirit is not just in accordance with rejecting the prophetic words that He is speaking in the "now moment" but rejecting the words He spoke in the written Word of God. Sometimes we think the prophetic and the written Word are separate, but they are not at all and should never be.

The prophetic utterance does not operate separately from the written Word because it originates from the same source. Jesus is "the Word that became flesh and lived among us," and there is no contradiction in Him. The oneness of the Trinity means that there is no separateness in thinking. Every prophetic revelation we truly receive from the Holy Spirit will fortify and strengthen what is in the Word.

The Holy Spirit longs to awaken us to the power of the written Word of God because His role is to reveal who God is to us. He functions to make Jesus known, to bring to remembrance the words Jesus spoke, and to reveal the heart and mind of the Father. The Holy Spirit convicts of sin and righteousness and often does this by highlighting the ways of God in His Word. Sometimes we long for a prophetic word but we fail to recognize the power of the Word of God to build us up and fortify the weak areas in our lives; it is the plumbline for us to build with and will reveal where what we are building is moving off of His design. The Spirit wants to make the Scriptures alive and active in our lives so that we build in accordance with His way.

NO SEPARATION

Just as the *Rhema* and *Logos* words of God are not separate or contradictory but all in accordance with His nature, so we are not to live separate in ourselves. Jesus commanded us to love our God with all our heart, all our mind, and all our strength (see

Matthew 22:37). God wants to encounter all of our being and wants us to love Him back with it all. The Holy Spirit does not just want to encounter a part of us, but He dwells in and transforms all of us. God made us to be fully connected to Him body, soul, and spirit. The Gnostics believed that we could do sinful things with our flesh but still live purely in our spirit because those parts were separate. This led to great heresy and impure living. We are seeing this thought subtly permeate society again. We see this belief coming to the surface through culture saying that I can be made in one form on the outside but be another thing on the inside. That I can feel like I am a certain way and even though I was not designed that way I can live according to how I feel about myself instead of how I was created. God designed us with great intention, and every part of you was made for Him and by Him. We will never find full freedom in altering ourselves or the truth to fit with how we feel, but instead we need to submit ourselves to the transformational power of the Spirit to align us with the perfect intention of our Father's design and plan. It is in encountering the heart and will of the Father and His great love for us that we come into the fullness of freedom.

When my husband and I bought our first house, we lived on a tight budget, so furnishing our house was something that took time. There is a store here that sells really inexpensive furniture that requires at-home assembly, and something I have really rebelled against in my existence is reading instruction manuals. They feel so tedious and overcomplicated to me. For someone who likes communication and clarity as much as I do, you would think I'd have an appreciation for written instructions, but I find it takes so long to get through them and I can't always understand them—which drives me crazy.

I remember one day going shopping and buying several bookshelves, a few side tables, and some nightstands and arriving home to have an assembly party that night. After dinner, my husband and I sat down to start putting these items together. Instead of wading through the instructions, I tried to assemble my items without prior planning or preparation. My husband, on the other hand, had read his instructions meticulously. I started assembly way before Ryan did, and looked like I was making good progress while Ryan was still reading and laying out all the pieces and parts. Though I seemed way ahead of him, I got to a point where I was stuck. I tried every which way to solve my problem, but eventually came to the conclusion I was missing a part, blaming the manufacturer for the issue. Frustrated, I gave up, deciding we would need to take it back and get the right pieces from the store. I took it all apart while my husband happily finished his piece.

After Ryan got done with his piece, he came over to look at my project, picked up the manual, and started laying all the pieces out. I of course told him he was wasting his time because there was no way we had everything we needed. After a bit of time, Ryan started trying to assemble the pieces together, following the manual I had no patience to read. You can, of course, get where I am going. Ryan had no problem assembling the item and all the pieces were in fact there. My neglecting to understand the intention and plan of the manufacturer left me arriving at the conclusion that there must have been an error in the packaging process of this item. In reading the instructions, my husband came to the revelation that I was wrong because I did not take the time to learn from the creator of the product.

I see this happen far too often because we have no connection with the Creator, His heart, intent, or His instructions, and we make up our own conclusions. I felt validated when I concluded "they" made a mistake, but I was in fact mistaken. My feelings were powerful but they were not truthful. My thoughts followed the path of least resistance and agreed with my feelings as though they were facts. That is scary to me. Too often we come to conclusions about ourselves separate from the intention and heart of our Designer and Creator. And in the same breath, far too often, we come to conclusions about God that are not accurate about Him. I can, without hesitation, say that my encounter with God completely shaped my way of thinking about God and myself. The Holy Spirit did what only He can do; He revealed the thoughts of God to me (see 1 Corinthians 2:10-12) and showed me the error in my thinking. The Spirit and the Word bring conviction of our true and authentic design, and in the changing of our mind (repentance) toward His thoughts and ways, we truly receive full freedom.

We cannot portion ourselves out to give an aspect and withhold another and expect to live in freedom. All of us are required. A life yielded to the Spirit enables us to love, crave, and abide in the Word of God and have His Word abide in us.

Encountering the Holy Spirit is foundational to us walking out powerful, bold faith in this Christian life. It was an encounter with the Spirit in Acts that birthed the Church and filled them with the ability to walk in the ways Jesus had called them to.

Holy Spirit, we recognize that we need You. We need You to encounter us to open our eyes to the reality that we don't battle against flesh and blood but against powers and principalities. We need clarity of our spiritual vision so that we might walk in bold faith in who Jesus is and what He has done. Thank You, Holy Spirit, that You strengthen our inner man to receive the mighty outpouring of God's supernatural love that establishes us in Christ. Jesus, help us to love others as You do, to see others as You see them, and to believe in them as You do.

Holy Spirit, would You draw us toward the Word of God? May we encounter the nature of God in His Word. Cultivate a hunger in our hearts to seek more of You in the Word. Reveal to us the beauty and victory of Jesus and our need for You as we read the letter You wrote for us to live and abide by. God, we don't want to live by our agenda or emotions, but we want to live surrendered to Your Spirit, aligned with Your truth that sets us free, and empowered by Your grace. Teach us, we pray. We must know You. Encounter us with Your presence and fill us with the full measure of Yourself. In Jesus's name we pray this. Amen.

CHAPTER 8

JESUS SPEAKING OF THE HOLY SPIRIT

The passages of John 14, 15, 16, and 17 are some of my most favorite in the Bible. These chapters are written consecutively as a conversation Jesus is having with His disciples about His leaving, and He reveals a very powerful piece of the story of God that is to unfold. This powerful revelation will be part of a new era that humanity will enter into—a life filled with the abiding presence of God, His Spirit now dwelling in us.

In the preceding passage, John 13, Jesus is speaking to His disciples about the time of His death that is approaching and the fact that He will be leaving them. This is a very distressing message He is giving to them, but He goes on to begin to share His prayer and purposes for them once the season shift happens. In the midst of it, in John 14:16, He gives them the promise of the Holy Spirit, whom He calls the *Paraclete*. This Greek word means "the one who is called alongside." There is no one word to really sum up the meaning of this word, but a few that scholars have used to translate the meaning of *Paraclete* are *Comforter, Counselor, Helper, Intercessor,* and *Advocate.* Jesus in John 14:16

shares how He will send "another" *Paraclete*, which does not mean someone "different" but one "the same as." This word describes that Jesus Himself had been the disciples' Comforter, Helper, Counselor, and Advocate while on earth. And now that He is physically leaving, He will send another just like Him, and it will be the Spirit of God.

Jesus's teaching on the promise of the Spirit is prophesying a brand-new epoch season for the people of God that is just around that corner for them.

> *However, I am telling you nothing but the truth when I say it is profitable (good, expedient, advantageous) for you that I go away. Because if I do not go away, the Comforter (Counselor, Helper, Advocate, Intercessor, Strengthener, Standby) will not come to you [into close fellowship with you]; but if I go away, I will send Him to you [to be in close fellowship with you]* (John 16:7 AMPC).

Jesus knows that His assignment on earth is coming to an end and He (fully God who put on flesh in submission to the will of the Father) will be leaving them. No longer will He live and walk with them as He has been for the last three years, because when He has completed His assignment here on earth, Jesus will ascend to the right hand of the Father and release the Holy Spirit; and when He does the power and presence of Jesus will go throughout the world dwelling in every believer. The Holy Spirit will come upon them on Pentecost and for the first time be poured out upon the disciples and fill them with the power of God to spread the Good News.

OUR COMFORTER

Although Jesus finds immense hope in the coming of the Spirit, can you imagine the distress the disciples are feeling as Jesus tells them of His coming death and departure from their presence? They have given up everything they know for the last three years and followed their Rabbi, whom they know is the Messiah. All their hope is in Him for the freedom and salvation of the Jews, and they are looking to His every move, every day.

Jesus knows they are distressed, but He doesn't change the subject because He also knows that what is to come is all part of a bigger plan—a glorious and victorious plan.

I'm sure the disciples thought the best way forward would be for Jesus to remain with them, becoming king and bringing an end to the rule of the Roman Empire. Surely Jesus dying was not the best option. How often in our lives do we feel distressed or worried about things? About something that is happening or not happening? How often do we feel like "That cannot be the best plan, Lord"?

The beauty of this moment is that Jesus lets them know that He will not leave them as orphans, nor will He ever leave us. We have a secure promise in the Lord that we will not be abandoned in our worst season or in our trials, and we certainly won't be abandoned when it doesn't make sense to us.

The comforting response Jesus seeks to give is not one of "it's going to be easy," but it is in the promise of the Holy Spirit that He gives hope. The promise of His ever-constant presence with them. Jesus doesn't hand them a strategy in this moment; He promises them the one who is present always, the one who is Comforter, Counselor—His very Spirit.

THE COMFORTER AND COURAGE

There was a season a few years ago when the Lord was dealing with me finding comfort in having control. The Lord told me, "You will cling to what you find comfort in," meaning that you begin to rely on what you find comfort in. Not all things that feel comforting are from God, nor do they give us freedom. In fact, some of the unhealthy things we find comfort in create more fear, anxiety, and hopelessness. Yes, there may be momentary relief, but the long-term fruit is destruction of everything good.

Finding comfort in control felt good when I had the ability to control, but we all know that is short-lived. All of a sudden, you are living a life filled with anxiety because you are trying to cling to things that are impossible to grip. An example is trying to control a loved one's happiness. On our best day we could be close to everything they need and fill every gap we could think of, but still sometimes that would not shift their mood. This would either lead to strife and frustration in our connection because they weren't responding to all our hard work the way we expected them to. Or it would lead to us overworking till we could not give anymore. At this point you are tired, frustrated, and feeling more powerless than before, and that is the place where offense and bitterness try to creep in.

These false places of comfort (like the need to feel in control) create chaos in our lives, but God invites us to find comfort in Him as our source. When we cling to God, we rely on His strength and truth, and in that we receive His courage.

When a toddler starts to explore the world for the first time, you will notice them, after a little exploration, run back to their mom or dad (or a close adult in their life) and get a hug or need to be picked up. After some time with Mom or Dad, they will venture back out to explore and grow and adventure. When our children receive comfort from the source of love in their lives, they receive courage. My youngest son just turned two years old, and he is the biggest adventurer in our family. He likes taking big risks, climbing things too high for my liking, and loves to jump and tumble. He is incredibly resilient and full of life and energy. What I find interesting, however, is that he is my child who needs the most comfort from me or my husband. He loves to be held or joyfully wrestled with. He needs my physical presence to replenish his courage tank, and from there he launches into his exploits.

This is not just a good idea or concept that I am speaking of here. We see the physical evidence of the Comforter (*Paraclete*) giving courage in the same way in the first few chapters of Acts.

In Matthew 26:30-35, we see Peter the disciple have a dialogue with Jesus about betrayal and denial. Peter, who I believe was honest and had a heart that deeply loved Jesus, is vehemently disagreeing with Jesus and saying that he would never deny Jesus, even in the face of death. I believe Peter here—I think he was being completely truthful in his desire. However, I know myself, and I know that it's easier to speak courageously than it is to act at times.

Peter was a man of zeal. We see him as the only one getting out of the boat to walk to Jesus on water (see Matthew 14:29), he cuts of the soldier's ear off when they come to arrest Jesus (see John 18:10), and he is one of two who run to see the empty tomb in John 20:3. But sadly, when the rubber met the road for him, when he faced the possibility of death or persecution after Jesus was arrested, he fell short of his promise to the Lord.

> *Now they arrested Him and led Him away, and brought Him to the house of the high priest; but Peter was following at a distance. After they kindled a fire in the middle of the courtyard and sat down together, Peter was sitting among them. And a slave woman, seeing him as he sat in the firelight, and staring at him, said, "This man was with Him as well." But he denied it, saying, "I do not know Him, woman!" And a little later, another person saw him and said, "You are one of them too!" But Peter said, "Man, I am not!" And after about an hour had passed, some other man began to insist, saying, "Certainly this man also was*

with Him, for he, too, is a Galilean." But Peter said, "Man, I do not know what you are talking about!" And immediately, while he was still speaking, a rooster crowed. And then the Lord turned and looked at Peter. And Peter remembered the word of the Lord, how He had told him, "Before a rooster crows today, you will deny Me three times." And he went out and wept bitterly (Luke 22:54-62 NASB).

I remember last year at a Good Friday service they were reading this portion of Scripture, and I was overtaken by the presence of God and a holy fear came over me as I began to realize how much like Peter I am. How there have been times when in zeal I have made promises to the Lord, but because of how the fear of man was allowed to operate in my life, so many times I denied Him in the face of fear. I think so often I can read the story of Peter and look down on him for his denial, perhaps because my denial doesn't seem as obvious or as big as his. But this Good Friday service showed me places where my heart did just as he had done. I see myself in Peter. I see humanity in Peter. I have told the Lord that He can have all of me, many times, and I truly felt like I meant it. I have promised Him my "yes" no matter what the cost, and then in the moments when He asked me to declare a truth or step out in faith I have let my fear of people break these promises I made.

But the story doesn't end there.

In Acts 2, the disciples receive the baptism of the Holy Spirit, the moment when the presence of God comes crashing in on the world, and for the first time in history He "fills the whole house." The coming of the Holy Spirit revealed a new era—God in us. The fullness of God, of His power, of His love, of His personhood available to us without restraint. Something marvelous happens to our dear friend Peter when he gets filled with the Holy Spirit—he becomes outrageously bold.

Peter preaches in Acts 2 with great boldness and begins to lead in the birth and the explosive expansion of the Gospel and thus the Church. In Acts 3 and 4, you see Peter and John walking in signs and wonders and facing persecution for it, but instead of Peter shrinking back in the face of persecution (as he had done previously), he cries out to the Lord for more boldness. What happens? He receives the Comforter who by His very presence produces courage.

The presence of Jesus gives us all courage. Courage doesn't come from us working ourselves into a frenzy or beating ourselves up for how I have failed in the past. Courage is not something I am either born with or not. It comes from surrendering my lack, my struggles to the Lord. Allowing God to hold and embrace us when we feel afraid and want to run away. The presence of God, the Holy Spirit, is the answer to everything we lack and He is ready to embrace us in our need and fill us to overflowing.

When we surrender our areas of weakness, fear, or lack to the Lord, He responds by filling that place with Himself, and we become immensely more courageous than we ever have been in our whole lives.

I have experienced this over and over again in my own life as I have yielded to the Holy Spirit. I spent a large part of my early ministry wanting to run away and find a place with less public exposure or pressure. I would daydream about an easier life, one with less fear, one that felt like I could do it with less dependence and vulnerability. But since my encounter with the Holy Spirit and the revelation of who He is to me, everything has fundamentally changed. When intimidation and fear of man comes and knocks on the door of my heart, trying to convince me to back down and self-protect, I no longer have the desire to welcome it into my life because I know there is no freedom there but more because I have found the one who is courage. Though, at times, I feel way over my head, I know He will never leave me. I have felt His incredible love, and the power of His availability to me, and that encourages me immensely. I still have to choose to live in the revelation I have received. When I feel overwhelmed my gut reaction is to work harder, as it feels counter intuitive as an adult that I would pause to be held by the Lord. But as I stop just to make myself aware of the Holy Spirit with me, and I invite Him to once again fill me and hold me in His presence. Right there in that place is where my true courage is found. That revelation of the power of God is mine to steward now and I will not trade it for anything.

Right now, I would love for you to take a moment with the Lord. Pause. Invite Him to come closer, and ask Him if there is anything that He would like you to surrender to Him, a place where He is inviting you to be held in His arms, so He can give you courage where you have been afraid.

Ask Him what He wants to be for you in this area. Your shield? Your reward? Your present Helper in a time of need? Power? Strength?

Let Him convict you if you need to lay some things down, and respond to His kindness with repentance exchanging any lies for God's truth. Let Him come to you in that place. Now invite Him into the place, the space you have carved out for Him to fill. He is with you!

THE ONE WHO COMES ALONGSIDE

In the way Jesus walked alongside the disciples, the Lord wants us to know that we can walk with Him in the same way because His very presence, His Spirit, is with us. The Holy Spirit delights in bringing comfort, strength, truth, and hope into every area of our lives. It is His joy to come alongside us and empower us to live a life in the fullness of God's promises.

As I have ventured into this intimate relationship with the Holy Spirit, He has truly become my best friend. When the Spirit of God came crashing into my life, I was deeply convicted of my approach toward Him. He is no assistant to my life or simple sideline helper to reach out to when stuck, but He also delights in helping us. The heart that treasures the Holy Spirit will also know how valuable He is in bringing aid. He delights in His role. The help and aid of the Holy Spirit in our lives is no small feat. It is the very same power exerted when He raised Christ from the dead and seated us in heavenly places that comes to our rescue (see Ephesians 1:20). What kind of "support" is that? It is immeasurable and beyond what we could deserve, and He loves to be our Helper, Intercessor, and the one who comes alongside. The introduction of the Spirit as the Helper in John 14, becomes the spring board for Jesus explaining some of the various functions and outcomes of union with Him. As we read through the next chapters, we see what the Holy Spirit makes possible for us as believers.

THE ABIDING

In John 15, Jesus begins to give us keys for fruitfulness in the Kingdom—to abide in Him, the true vine, and He in us. Jesus's Spirit is soon going to be released to fill the lives of those who come into faith in Him as the Savior, and this is going to enable us to not simply be with Him but for Him to abide in us and us in Him. Acts 17:28 (NIV) says that it is *"in him we live and move and have our being."*

What an incredible new reality—that we can live in such connection and intimacy that He can live in us and us in Him. This is made possible by the release of His Spirit. Living in proximity to Jesus was so incredibly transformational, powerful, and catalytic in the disciples' lives. Men went from ordinary vocations as fishermen, tax collectors, and doctors to living as followers of God in flesh. The great demonstrations of the power of the Spirit flowing through the life of Jesus and experiencing God as a Father would have been completely life-transforming, and yet Jesus was saying there was a deeper intimacy to come for all who believe. We as believers long for closeness with the Lord, we were designed for it, and God desires it even more than we do. Jesus sending the Spirit from the Father was the context in which abiding could be taught. Jesus is teaching a new reality for these men of God. He is saying, "As I have been living in oneness with the Father, by the Spirit so you will be able to."

The giving of the Spirit to believers is the open door for us to abide in Jesus. When we surrender our lives to Jesus and receive salvation because of His death and resurrection, we become the perfect vessel to host and cooperate with His Holy Spirit. The continuous awareness and welcome of our hearts to the Holy Spirit enables us to live a life that remains in Him and He in us. When we make room for the Lord in our lives, we welcome the operation of the Spirit in us so that we can live in union with Jesus. The context of what Jesus is teaching in John 15 all hinges on the release and reception of His Spirit. Without the gift of the Spirit of God, we cannot abide in Jesus and have Jesus abide in us. Because we have been so freely given the gift of salvation and have been washed clean and purified by Jesus's blood, we can now host the most holy one, the very Spirit of God, and it is His Spirit that makes abiding in Him possible. If it is intimacy with the Lord that begets fruitfulness, then us posturing ourselves to encounter Him in our daily lives is the most powerful and productive choice we can make.

IT IS TO YOUR ADVANTAGE

Jesus states something so profound and perplexing to His friends in John 16:7. He says that "it is to your advantage that I should go." I am not sure about you, but if I was walking with Jesus I am not sure that I would feel like it was to my advantage that He leaves. But Jesus at this moment has a much broader understanding of the picture than the disciples have. Jesus understands what He is about to accomplish and who He is going to release; He understands the function of the Holy Spirit and how valuable He is to the birth and growth of the New Testament Church. There is no competitive comparison being made here, because the Holy Spirit does not operate on His own but is one with the Father and Son and operates in full cooperation with them.

I think we can superimpose our human beliefs on the Godhead and sometimes create a competition or false hierarchy, but they live in complete oneness and mutual submission to one another. The three persons of the Trinity are one God with the same nature and glory, but their roles in relating to the world differ.

Jesus knows His assignment, and He understands His role and the manifold work that the cross, resurrection, and His ascension will accomplish. He understands that victory is about to be won for His people and will make a way for all who receive Him as Christ to receive His Spirit to work powerfully in and through us, to manifest His victory over the enemy here on earth. Up until this point, His disciples have experienced Jesus at one place, at one time geographically, because, though fully God, He chose to put on flesh and live in that way with them for His specific purpose on earth. But this shift to the coming of His Spirit will release the power of Himself to fill all flesh across the globe. The presence and power of Jesus will now be available to go far and wide into every home, region, and people group.

This is incredibly profound, not just for then but for us all now. The indwelling of the Holy Spirit being available to us all is something the Church must grasp and, I dare to say, contend for until it becomes a walked-out reality in our day-to-day lives. The words *contend for* are challenging because they could be describing something that we don't yet have, and we all know that the Holy Spirit has been released, but just because He is available to us does not mean that we have grasped the true power of His presence with us. It is the hearts of those who will seek Him and trust Him that will have the eyes to see and ears to hear what He is doing and saying.

The Holy Spirit is with us always, to be hosted and partnered with in every area and facet of our lives. He is not limited to a Sunday service nor a church building but has been poured out for us all. Our church gatherings keep us connected to and aware of the fundamental truths of our faith, to the mighty power of God available to us, and to our responsibility within our covenant, but they are meant to be the launching point of our week into the world where we are fully aware of Christ who lives and dwells within us. A life lived in this reality is full of hope, victory, and Kingdom solutions because we live in the reality that our limitless King is with us.

TESTIFIES OF JESUS AND BRINGS TO REMEMBRANCE

When the Advocate comes, whom I will send to you from the Father—the Spirit of truth who goes out from the Father—he will testify about me. And you also must testify, for you have been with me from the beginning (John 15:26-27 NIV).

Just as Jesus celebrates the coming of the Spirit, whom He will send from the Father, the Spirit will have the joyous role to testify of Jesus and reveal Him to the world. When I encountered God in such a powerful and mysterious way, the work of the Holy Spirit in my life was that which profoundly magnified the worth of Jesus in my heart and mind. My deep love and value for the Spirit of God are because He began to reveal the beauty and majesty of Jesus and the nature of the Father in a way I had never known. He didn't testify of Himself but instead worked perfectly in my heart to reveal the Father and the Son rightly, thus revealing Himself to me too. I cannot adequately describe to you how precious the Holy Spirit is to me. He set the record straight for me on what I live my life by and who I live it for. Jesus's life was a model for us all to see what our life lived in surrender to the Lord could look like. The many demonstrations of miracles, signs, and wonders were for each of us a testimony of what our lives would look like in Him. When we face challenges in life, we have the choice to allow the life of Jesus to define our response or to allow our fear or unbelief to do so. The Holy Spirit is at work within us to nudge us toward faith in Jesus. He reminds us of what Christ did and what is available so that our experiences don't dictate our faith. If I do not see it in the life of Jesus, then I do not want to create a place for it to dwell in my heart.

To see Jesus rightly means we need a revelation of Him and what He has done, and for this we need the work of the Holy Spirit. The Gospel is simple but not necessarily easy. It is something we cannot simply grasp in our mind but must be apprehended in the spirit, and we must let it touch every fiber of our being. The reason it is not easy is because we live in the tension of the reality of the Kingdom available now and the not yet. We know Jesus has paid for it all but we have not seen it "all" manifest yet. We can find ourselves wanting to rationalize the tension of the now and the not yet, to remove the discomfort of having faith for something we feel we have no control in. The problem with this is we more often rationalize ourselves away from faith and risk instead of toward it. I don't want to talk my way out of a life lived in the power of the Holy Spirit. We cannot live by earthly knowledge alone; we need to turn to the Holy Spirit and allow Him to remind us of the wonder-working power in the death and life of Jesus and let Him awaken us to the one who speaks the words of the Spirit and life (see John 6:63). The Holy Spirit is sent to us so that we may enter into the great mystery of Christ in us, the hope of the glory (see Colossians 1:27) and what that means for our lives lived with Him daily.

There is much Jesus taught while He walked the earth, but not all was understood or received. There is much we have heard as believers in sermons, read in the Word, or sung in worship of Jesus, but not all remain in the forefront of our minds. The beautiful work of the Spirit is that He brings to remembrance all Jesus said, what we have read in the Word and encountered in Him, and that which we have received in Him (see John 14:26). The Spirit is the one who helps us remember and comprehend His wonderful truth and the great mysteries of His Kingdom.

SPIRIT OF TRUTH

I have many more things to say to you, but you cannot bear them at the present time. But when He, the Spirit of truth, comes, He will guide you into all the truth; for He will not speak on His own, but whatever He hears, He will speak; and He will disclose to you what is to come. He will glorify Me, for He will take from Mine and will disclose it to you. All things that the Father has are Mine; this is why I said that He takes from Mine and will disclose it to you (John 16:12-15 NASB).

SURRENDERED TO THE HOLY SPIRIT

Jesus is communicating in this passage that there is so much He still wants to give His followers, but He is aware they are unable to bear it. He has so much wealth and revelation of the value, function, and power of what His life, death, resurrection, and ascension will mean for them, but they cannot get a full grip on it in that moment. He finds comfort in sending the Spirit because He will glorify Jesus and give them in due time the deep treasures of revelation that Jesus carries and holds, as the Father gave.

The work of the Spirit expands our capacity to carry the knowledge and revelation of the Son of God that we so desperately need and quickens us to grasp the powerful mysteries of the Gospel so that we might be transformed by Him and walk in the ways of Jesus. The majesty and beauty of Jesus is just one facet of Him that would completely transform a life if engaged with just a fraction of it. What about His holiness? His might? His victory? The list goes on and on. All of Heaven cries "holy" as they behold Him; the twenty-four elders—people of such great stature that they are positioned around His throne—when they see Jesus, they fall down at His feet and cast down their crowns, their symbols of authority, wisdom, and power. They do this because all the glory of their lives pales in comparison to the great glory of God.

It is the greatest delight for the Holy Spirit to work in us to aid us in connecting with that which we have not been able to bear in other seasons. The work of the Spirit drives a deep obsession for the value of our desperate need for Jesus and a hunger to know the Father. The Holy Spirit is constantly leading and guiding to the feet of Jesus as we walk through life's circumstances. It is at His feet that every lofty argument or assaulting word of the enemy is brought under submission to the obedience of Christ (see 2 Corinthians 10:5).

The value of Christ to our lives, in our lives, and what He has done for us is so magnificent and wide and deep and high it is hard to comprehend. In Jesus Christ, all things hold together (see Colossians 1:18). That means that there is nothing visible or invisible that is beyond our need of Him. When the Holy Spirit began to reveal the overwhelming need, value, and desire my being had for Jesus, the darling of Heaven, many things I thought I had needed grew dim in this knowledge of who He is, was, and will be to me. Things that felt complicated or convoluted in my life became unusually simple. The list of my responsibilities and priorities became whittled down to one thing: "What is God saying about this?" The Holy Spirit awoke me to the preciousness and the perfection of the Lord's leadership. The striving to be everything to those around me ceased in the reality that Jesus was everything to us all. People often ask how I balance ministry, family, travel, and my many responsibilities, but the truth is that I am not trying to balance them all nor am I trying to meet everyone's needs. I am trying to follow the leadership of the Lord in my life and allow Him to order my steps. This is something Bill has shared with us many times and it was in the Holy Spirit meeting me so powerfully that the truth of Jesus being enough for everything I needed became true and a lived-out reality in my life. This doesn't mean I never get overwhelmed or miss the mark; it simply means that when I do, I get to go back to the Lord and invite His leadership in the places of anxiety, and it is there that I find His peace.

Something I have come to realize is that there is the confusion and at times the fear around the Holy Spirit. Because the Spirit of God is not tangible for the human mind to conceive, we have created our own thoughts around who He is and what He does. For many it is easier to relate to God the Father because we have all had an experience with fathers in our lifetime, and the same with Jesus because He walked in our shoes for a time. But when it comes to the Spirit of God, we tend to shy away from talking about Him because it feels more physically intangible and something not as easily grasped.

This is very similar to how we would feel comfortable talking about our physical needs over our emotional needs because one is more tangible. For example, asking for a glass of water at someone's home feels more simple and less vulnerable than expressing a need for eye contact or a hug, and yet both are needs—one just more physically tangible than the other.

Everything about our relationship with the Holy Spirit is vulnerable and incredibly intimate. He is the abiding presence of God within us. Our invitation to the Holy Spirit requires surrender of being in full control and invites Him to do a work in us that we haven't been able to accomplish on our own. And as we have said before, that kind of surrender is one of complete trust. Trust and surrender go hand in hand, and to have the

Spirit of God in full operation in our lives we must give both completely to the Lord. Giving up control personally and in a corporate setting feels daunting to many. The fear of man has subtly crept into our gatherings, and we have capped the work of the Spirit in the fear He would do something that may offend people. In this fear, and in other ways too, we have limited the movement of the Spirit and thus limited our connection and awareness to the majesty and glory of the Lord. We must not create a god in our image, who fits our mold and comfort level, instead of seeing Him as He is and for who He is. Our need to serve people and their preferences has too many times closed the doors to the work of the Spirit of God, limiting Him to our comfort and thus trading our inheritance in Him for form with no power. We do not need to entertain people; we need to lead them to the feet of Jesus, and nothing and no one does this better than the Holy Spirit.

The Holy Spirit is to be revered, honored, and hosted by His people without fear because He does not operate on His own. The Spirit does not glorify Himself but reveals only what the Father tells Him and glorifies Jesus our Lord (see John 16:13). I remember one evening meeting we had—during worship I was sobbing on the floor as the Spirit was revealing the value of the feet of Jesus. As I worshiped, I felt the weight of my need to serve Him and how it was aligning my heart to serve others. I sobbed as I clung to His feet and recognized how much I needed to be in this position as a minister and pastor. The feet of Jesus revealed the posture that I was called to—serving at His feet. My sobbing at His feet then became sobs of gratitude as I realized that the Holy Spirit, by His mercy, was allowing me to step into that powerful truth because He loved me and longed for me to know Jesus.

The revelation of the value and worth of Jesus is not relegated to moments but is available to those who live in friendship with the Spirit. The heart's welcome to the Spirit is a welcome to see Jesus rightly, a welcome to have Jesus glorified and magnified in your heart and mind and to know His ways and majesty. And when we behold Him, we are transformed into His likeness, and the likeness of Jesus is a glory too magnificent to describe. Seeing Jesus paints our world in vibrant colors of hope, joy, and peace. It gives meaning to valleys and mountaintops and sustains us through trials and victory. Dependance on the Holy Spirit is vital to see Jesus as we need to.

FRUIT AND GIFTS

I think the fear of the Spirit of God has at times come because man has overly focused on the gift instead of the fruit. The gifts of the Spirit are wonderful and valuable and must be treasured, but they must not be mistaken as fruit. Fruit is a by-product of the work of the Spirit in us (see Galatians 5:22), while gifts are freely given and not always connected to the condition of our heart. A tree cannot bear fruit under poor conditions, and thus there are conditions to us bearing fruit. No water, no nourishment equals no fruit. And thus, we as believers cannot bear the fruit of the God-life without remaining in connection with the Lord, feasting on the bread of life and hosting Him daily (see John 15:4). The fruit of our lives displays a life that has been and is being purified by the very presence of Jesus in operation in us. Purity is the evidence of His work (the refiner's fire) in us.

We have all been stung by someone operating in a gift but not in dependence on the Holy Spirit, and so at times we have dismissed the immense value of the Spirit because of the misuse of the gift. All gifts can be misused, and when they are they can cause pain and destruction, but when used properly they are incredibly powerful. My goal is not to emphasize misuse but to emphasize proper use. We must have both purity of heart and display God's mighty power, not one or the other. In fear of lack of purity, we shy away from teaching power. In watching the impure heart misuse a powerful truth (gift), we can back away from wielding that specific weapon altogether, when in fact God is looking for those pure in heart to demonstrate His intention of the gift. Those walking in communion with the Spirit bear not just gifts but also the fruit of the work of the Holy Spirit in their lives. To be people of incredible purity but also walk in the power of God, we need to remain connected to the vine.

As an illustration, I cannot shy away from teaching my children, as they become teenagers, the power of their sexuality. If I do, I diminish the value of purity and their responsibility in the stewardship of this. Why would purity matter if their sexuality was not powerful? Purity matters because sexuality is incredibly powerful; when used correctly it knits a marriage together, makes two people one, and bonds them in the spirit like no other relationship they will experience in their lifetime. When there is no control or limit, it will produce life and legacy, regardless of whether we want it to or not. God created the power of our sexuality to be contained in the structure of the covenant of marriage. When our sexuality is managed in purity and we keep it in the confines of marriage, it is healthy and life-giving, but when we experience it without purity it is destructive.

Purity is vital for the structure that will carry power. There is no way to see the Kingdom come on earth as it is in Heaven without the demonstration of the power of Jesus. If Jesus only walked in purity on the earth, there would have been no miracles. In contrast, if Jesus only demonstrated power and no purity, there would be no validity in the miracle. He did both perfectly and calls us to yield our lives to His work in us to do the same, only He will perfect it in us.

These chapters in John that we have glanced at paint an incredible picture of what is going to be possible for every believer because of the infilling of the Holy Spirit. The Holy Spirit is the one who is going to make communion with God a reality for every believer. The Spirit is going to afford us to be connected to the Father and allow us to remain in God in such a way that we could bear the fruit of His Kingdom and His righteousness. I would love to encourage you to go and read all four chapters (John 14, 15, 16 and 17) and highlight what you see the Word is saying is possible because we have received the Holy Spirit. I pray that these passages stir a hunger in you for more of Him and awaken you to the power of a life lived in connection with the Spirit of God.

CHAPTER 9

THE AVAILABILITY OF
THE HOLY SPIRIT

INTIMACY OVER OUTCOME

For the last few years, I have spent much of my time sharing my story in the context of the Lord breaking off the fear of man in my life. The Lord led me to speak about this as it was one of the most powerful transformations I received from this encounter with the Holy Spirit. I think many people can relate to the effects of the fear of man in their life. I'm not sure anyone could say that they have never experienced the fear of man in one way or another.

Though the fruit of this encounter with the Holy Spirit has been so impactful in my life (and He purposed for it), there is something that was even more precious than the outcome. When God encountered me the way He did, I didn't know quite what He was doing at that moment, but one thing I knew for certain was that He was with me.

Often when God begins to move in a tangible way in our lives, we are quick to try and figure out what it is for. We want to figure it out so we can move forward. I find that we as humans find it challenging to simply experience something without knowing "why."

As I said before, I am an overseer in the School of Supernatural Ministry here in Redding, California. Over the last six months, we have been enjoying a beautiful outpouring of the Spirit in which many of our students have been experiencing prolonged encounters with the Holy Spirit as I did just a few years ago. Many times, these students will come to me and other leaders in our environment who have had experiences with the Holy Spirit and ask us questions about what God is trying to accomplish through the encounter. Though this is not a bad question to be asking, the outcome is not the primary reason for the encounter. *Nearness is.*

CONNECTION AND RELATIONSHIP

Think about when you are in a connected relationship—it could be a best friend, family member, or spouse. When we experience meaningful connection, it is seldom because we are trying to produce something. Instead, we are purposing to be close. Pressure to produce is one of the greatest enemies of true passion. When you get locked into the idea that a certain achievement or outcome is what makes it successful, intimacy wanes. When connection and greater understanding of one another are what we define as success, intimacy increases. Seeking connection means I seek to know you instead of trying to get somewhere with you. When we seek to know God for who He is and not what He does, we receive the full benefit.

I remember when I became a mom. For the first time in my life, someone else was completely dictating my day-to-day activities. I remember days feeling completely overwhelmed because I had what I thought I should accomplish on my agenda but I simply could not get to all of it. I remember feeling like a failure at the end of the day because I had nothing to show for the hours I had spent at home. Before having a little one, I could get so much done, and now I just felt like I couldn't keep up. One day I sat with the Lord and began asking Him about this. He said one thing to me: "Forget not the benefits." I knew at that moment the Lord was reminding me that there were benefits in the assignment He had given me that I was missing out on.

As I began to look at this, I started asking the Holy Spirit, "Where are the benefits You have given me?" What I began to see was that all the benefits were hidden in connection to this little human who seemed to be disrupting all my tasks. The joy for my soul in that season was not going to be from the outcome but from pursuing a relationship with my son. When I leaned into joy in our connection and focused on being present to the new human in my life, the other things slotted in after. When I started to focus on connection with my God-given role in that season, my soul was reenergized to accomplish tasks in the context of the right priorities.

But seek first the kingdom of God and his righteousness, and all these things will be added to you (Matthew 6:33 ESV).

We know that encountering the Holy Spirit provides a wonderful outcome, but knowing that can cause us to prioritize the outcome over the connection (encounter) with Him. In other words, sometimes our knowledge of the benefits of seeking the Kingdom can actually become a distraction to seeking the Kingdom itself. Though all things will be added to us when we seek first His Kingdom, we can get sidetracked and get the priority mixed up. When our focus moves to all things added, then we have neglected to put seeking Him in the first place.

SEEKING HIS HANDS

Encounters reprioritize our lives. They establish God in His rightful place, and wrong thinking is addressed. In my encounter, the Lord addressed a mindset that I repented of many times. I remember recognizing that too often we come seeking His hands and not His face or His feet.

In this dialogue with the Lord, I understood His hands represent His provision of gifts, anointing, favor, etc.—all things the Lord wants to give to us in abundance. His feet represented His lordship in our lives and our position as servants. His face is intimacy and connection. I want to share that there is a great tension in what I am saying because ultimately God wants to bless us abundantly and He also wants the Christian life to walk in the lavish outpouring of His hands. He loves giving us gifts; Jesus loves touching our lives, and He paid for all the benefits we receive from His hands. He wants us to seek Him and demonstrate His miracle-working power and love to the world. Loving the Lord's feet and face was a shift I felt was needed to seek first what was in His heart and what His agenda was, and that would ultimately bring the mighty and wonderous work of His hands. When we seek His hands first, we are looking for the benefit without the cost, intimacy without covenant. God is not a transactional God; He is a God of the covenant, and He keeps every promise. The Christian life is one that is not just a demonstration but also one of deep love and servanthood.

Just like in a loving marriage, we don't seek a spouse to wash dishes, repair the car, mow the lawn, or fold the laundry—though they may do all those things. We seek a spouse for lifelong connection and partnership. In the loving partnership that we build with one another, we receive immensely, and it is designed that way. But one is prioritized.

We have the knowledge of the Spirit and His gifts, but do we know His nature and His personhood? One of my deepest concerns is that we would be trained to operate in the gifts of the Spirit, but do we actually know the Person of Spirit Himself?

Before my encounter, I used to believe the gift of prophecy was to benefit the person I was prophesying over—that they were receiving a gift. But because of the radical intimacy I experienced in my encounter with Him, I began to realize I had completely missed it. The first miracle of the gift of prophecy is that God is speaking to me. That His very own Spirit is whispering His heart and intentions to me, and He feels that I can be entrusted with what He cares about. Now, of course the person receiving is getting a gift, but that is secondary to the profound truth that the King of Glory tells His secrets and mysteries to His friends.

May we operate in power in the gifts of God and bless others abundantly, but may it always be from a place of intimacy with Him and seeking to know God in all of His ways.

Psalm 25:14 (NASB):

> *The secret of the Lord is for those who fear Him, and He will make them know His covenant.*

Or in the English Standard Version:

> *The friendship of the Lord is for those who fear him, and he makes known to them his covenant.*

THE HOLY SPIRIT REVEALS

When we seek God for His feet and face, we prioritize His lordship and His friendship and we invite His revelation in our lives. Revelation is not simply a tool, it is one of the manifestations of the work of the Holy Spirit (see Isaiah 11:4). In Ephesians

1:17, Paul talks about the Holy Spirit as the spirit of wisdom and revelation. The Spirit of God reveals to us the mysteries of God and revelations of our inheritance in Jesus, but He wants to be pursued because of love not because of function.

THE PERSON OF THE HOLY SPIRIT

When I say the Holy Spirit is a Person, I don't mean that He is flesh and blood; I mean to define Him as a being with "a will, a mind, and emotions." Though the Holy Spirit can be fire, oil, wind, rain, revelation, wisdom, a dove, etc., that does not mean He is relegated to a function to be "used." Just as me being a mother, daughter, pastor, preacher, etc. does not relegate me simply to my function either. I remain Hayley in all those functions above, and the essence of my personhood flows through each of those functions.

We see this "personhood" in Scripture. The mind of the Holy Spirit is spoken of in Romans 8:27 as He advocates in intercession. The evidence of the will of the Spirit is seen in many places, one being when He led Jesus into the wilderness in Matthew 3 to be tested and fortified for His ministry. Again, in Acts 15:28 we see the Holy Spirit wills and purposes certain things to happen. And finally, we see He has emotions when Paul asks us not to grieve Him in Ephesians 4:30.

THE HOLY SPIRIT HAS MADE HIMSELF VULNERABLE TO OUR LONGING

Encounters with the Holy Spirit awaken us to the profound reality that God is fully available to us without any hesitation. Like the never-ending flow of a waterfall, that is the response of the Spirit to His Bride. I think we have believed a lie that God is distant from us or waiting for us to jump through hoops in order to be available to us. But the truth is that God is fully available to us and He has made every provision for the fullness of Him to live in the fullness of us. But do we realize it? An example of this is having a completely full bank account but not knowing how to withdraw from it.

When we start to think of the complete availability of the Spirit of God, we must become aware that there is a vulnerability He has chosen to live in constantly. Think about the people you love the most. The people we love the most and are loyal to are the ones we are most vulnerable to because we are most available to them. The availability that we live with to the people with whom we are in covenant makes us more susceptible to getting wounded because we don't have a shield up against them.

We must not mistake the Spirit's grief or ability to be affected by our response for insecurity. He is mighty God; He is powerful beyond measure and is completely confident in His nature. His love is steadfast and does not waver, no matter how many times we do.

But because of His great love for us He will never shield Himself from us. The nature of God is immovable. He is not like us. He does not turn from us, but we can turn from Him. Faithful is His nature, which means it is what He is at His core and so He has chosen to live vulnerable to our response.

In my encounter many times I experienced a deep ache in my heart that I knew was the grief of the Holy Spirit. It was the ache of a heart that was longing to be with those He loved to fulfill and empower them. I felt pain as I realized He had been waiting patiently for me to be ready for what He had wanted to pour out on me for so long. Though there is no instability in Him, His beckoning was for my sake and benefit. I am deeply saddened by this reality because He is far too precious for us to reject.

The Holy Spirit is sensitive, and His presence and personhood must be treasured. His function is to come alongside, and so He will always be reaching out to us. This is one of the reasons why we are cautioned about quenching and grieving Him.

GRIEF AND QUENCHING

Just as we can grieve His heart, we can also quench Him. When we shield ourselves from the operation of the Holy Spirit and rebel against Him, we grieve His heart. Rebellion is moral failing, but it is also willfully rejecting His ways and choosing our own.

I personally don't enjoy talking about this because I think the reality of His availability is far more exciting than our missteps. But we would be doing Him a great disservice if we did not acknowledge this. I am concerned about how willing we are to have meetings without dependence on the Spirit of God. Acknowledgment of His presence is not *dependence*; it's a seat at the table, but not the high seat of honor He deserves.

We quench the Holy Spirit when we limit His working in us. Our fear of disappointment, our own self-reliance, and our unwillingness to trust the Lord in all we do shield us from the movement of His presence in our lives. There are times when we hold the Spirit of God at arm's length because we are busy trying to accomplish something, forgetting His incredible strength and availability to us.

We can quench the Spirit personally, but we can also quench Him corporately when we limit His movement and operation in the midst of our gatherings. When we immediately try to attach a purpose to why He is moving without first enjoying the fact that we are experiencing the Person of God in our midst, we miss the first priority of our relationship. Intimacy.

I have learned that when the manifest presence of God's Spirit is at work, it is not the time for me to add too many words but simply find out what He is doing and ask for more. Seeking for what He is doing is in order to partner with and honor His leading versus seeking for the purpose in that is often more attached to the outcome and benefit we will receive. We will, of course, receive so much benefit from God moving and breathing in our midst, but I want to seek to love Him rather than the benefits of being in His love. Loving the Lord and seeking Him first will bring all the benefits. When the Holy Spirit begins to evidently touch someone I am praying for, I quickly shift from prophetic words or prayers to blessing what He is doing and asking for more. My goal is not to add in that moment but to partner with Him, because when His hands are working on someone I surely cannot bring any more to that moment than He already is. Trying to add "my piece" to the moment can at times detract from what the Spirit is doing and cause the person who is receiving to try and "listen" to my words instead of receive that which we have no words for. As I soften my heart and give attention to what He is doing, our movements become unified and all other distractions fade. This allows my faith and the faith of the person receiving ministry to be single in focus and attach itself to the power of what the Holy Spirit is doing, and it inevitably increases how much we receive.

I have realized that He is far too precious to be squandered and He will wait humbly for the place He is due. The vigilance and humility required of us to make room for God to move in our hearts are the very things we need to have built in us to host Him well. Learning to recognize the work of the Spirit teaches me to cooperate with the anointing—and recognize the Spirit of God is the anointing itself.

YIELDING TO THE MEETING

To encounter the Holy Spirit is not to encounter a thing but a Person—one who has emotions, intentions, and longing. If we don't understand this, then encounters are not something to be treasured or valued. But if we grasp it, we are not simply shaking but we are being physically touched by God, and that is holy. I have too often moved in human wisdom when the Lord starts to move because I have seen it as a "happening" instead of Him moving. When we do this, we can rush in and try to adjust it to what we feel comfortable with. When someone encounters the Person of the Holy Spirit, they encounter the living God, and we must be careful not to be quick to judge the moment. Of course, we need a healthy community and discernment, but sometimes we need to take a step back and ensure we are not letting fear or our preference "lens" these moments.

The very fact that God is completely available to us tells me that He *desires* you not because He lacks anything but because you were created for Him and by Him. If you long for more of God, which I'm sure you do, you must know that even more He longs for all of you. The fullness of God deeply desires to fill the fullness of you. This is a very interesting concept for our flesh to grasp. First, it's tough because we struggle to believe that God would want to inhabit our flesh. But under the blood of Jesus, we become sanctified, and so we are made holy habitation when we live submitted to Jesus. The other challenge with our flesh is that when the weight and power of God meet our mortal bodies, it is not often something we are in control of. When the Almighty God meets our fragile beings, it can be quite the collision.

When the Holy Spirit began to fill me as He did in January of 2020, it was not something that I would describe as pleasant or convenient. While it was the most wonderful experience of my whole life thus far, it required a full surrender of my flesh. There was nothing convenient about the way that God encountered me—but it changed me forever. Sometimes we can quench the Holy Spirit because when He comes in fullness, it isn't what we imagined nor what we think is convenient. I am sad to say it, but I feel at times we have had our hunger for the Holy Spirit on a leash. I weep as I write this because I could not think of anything more painful than constricting our expectation for the Spirit of God. When we want to keep God in the framework of our understanding, we shackle our receiving of Him and, in His grace, He waits for our readiness. We must not make Him wait. Of course, He is sovereign and He can move should He choose to, but He Himself is Love. Love is patient, it is long-suffering, and it keeps no record of wrongs. Therefore, there are times when He has been long-suffering in His patient waiting for us to be prepared for Him without limiting how He comes.

THE PRECIPICE OF OUTPOURING AND PRAYER

The Lord is postured toward us always, and He waits in anticipation of your gaze coming toward Him. I believe that we as the

Church are on the precipice of a mighty outpouring of the Holy Spirit. There is an invitation for us to enter the "upper room" and partner with deep prayer and intercession as we cry out for more of Him. The cry for "more" does not come because He is holding Himself back but simply because He wants the invitation of a vigilant Bride. The persistent widow is the picture of the prayer for revival (see Luke 18:1-8). Revival is when the very presence of God meets His people who have been crying out for Him. We are not crying out for a thing but for the very presence of Jesus, His very Spirit, poured out on us so we would awaken to His Kingdom. The one who is willing to set everything aside and persistently pray, I believe, is the one who receives great breakthrough.

Breakthrough is not a happenstance; it is the nature of God. The Holy Spirit brings breakthrough wherever He goes because it is simply who He is and therefore what He does. I have wondered how many times I have fallen short of experiencing a revival because I have not been willing to persist in longing for Him. Our longing is a landing strip for the power of the Spirit. When we partner with the Holy Spirit in intercession, He reveals Heaven's mandate and we get entrusted to be the delivery men and women to bring it to earth.

PERSISTENT PRAYER READIES US

Why persistent prayer? Persistent prayer develops us, it builds a foundation and a structure within us that is able to adequately hold and host His glory. Persistent prayer is not for God's benefit but for my benefit. Prayer aligns me with the heart of God. It is in the place of prayer that I commune with the Holy Spirit, and He reveals to me what Heaven is declaring. As I align with God, He builds in me a wineskin that is suitable for the outpouring of His presence. Our longing for God awakens our hearts to the things of God. As we allow ourselves to long for Him and to cry out for His presence, it shapes us and molds us to host Him well.

When we abort the cry for God, we neglect what the cry builds in us. The fear of disappointment shields us from the availability of the Holy Spirit to do a mighty work in us. To combat disappointment, we must once again surrender and trust in the Lord that He can shepherd us through any uncertainty. This requires leaning not on our own understanding but instead in all ways to acknowledge Him, right in the midst of us, as He straightens our paths and brings us to the place where we lack nothing (see Proverbs 3:5 and Psalm 24). Disappointment that remains un-surrendered to the Lord is like a wound that is not clean. Infection grows where disappointment goes ignored, but healing comes when we offer it to Him in prayer. This invitation allows the Spirit of God to begin to touch the places in our lives that we have shielded from Him. Prayer aligns us with His mind and heart and removes stumbling blocks in our paths. The presence of the Holy Spirit is precious and also so weighty and incredibly powerful. The weight of His presence cannot be placed on a foundation that is broken. Longing and desire for the Lord welcomes the healing work of the Holy Spirit to restore cracked foundations and fortify the walls of our vessel so that we can host more of Him so that we might see a mighty move of His Spirit among us.

As He longs for our longing hearts, it is not simply for His benefit. Really, it is for ours. Everything that God desires from us is because He knows we need it. God lacks nothing, but we need everything, and He is everything we need. Every process and journey yielded to the Spirit of God is used to build in us the capacity to host more of Him. The more we can host the Spirit, the more alive we become. He does it all for our benefit because He loves us. The Holy Spirit is available to us because He longs to be near to us because His nearness makes us alive. This is a generous God.

THE SPIRIT INTERCEDES FOR US

Now in the same way the Spirit also helps our weakness; for we do not know what to pray for as we should, but the Spirit Himself intercedes for us with groanings too deep for words; and He who searches the hearts knows what the mind of the Spirit is, because He intercedes for the saints according to the will of God (Romans 8:26-27 NASB).

As we come to the close of this chapter, I cannot help but feel the bubbling delight in the heart of the Holy Spirit as He reminds us that He intercedes when we cannot. He teaches us how to pray and gives us the language of Heaven to pray when we have no words. He is wooing us into a place of longing and will meet us there in our cry for more of God to teach us how to access the more. This is why He is so wonderful.

I will never forget the day I was preparing a message on the "Person of the Holy Spirit" and was writing about Him not being a tool to use, and He interrupted what I thought was a wonderful message to say, "Hayley, I love that you want people to not want Me for what I can do but for who I am, it is important, but please tell them I do love to be helpful. When fire is required, I love to set people ablaze for Jesus; and when it's time for oil, I love to be the Anointing and bring healing; and when it's time to refresh, I am the River. I want to be what My people need."

This is the best news. All these things we are deeply in need of, He is, and when we seek Him, we will find Him.

PRAYER IN RESPONSE

Holy Spirit, thank You for Your unwavering availability; thank You for making Yourself vulnerable to our invitation so that we might come to know the Lord Jesus. We long for You to fill us, to encounter us. Make us a resting place for you to dwell. Holy Spirit, we invite the fullness of You to fill every part of us. We must have revival, awaken us to reality of Your availability, and the beauty of your personhood. Make us hungry to know You. Forgive us if we have grieved your heart or quenched your moving. We need Your presence; teach us to host You well so that we can experience Your fullness. Make us lovers of the feet, Jesus; reveal to us the Master's face. Jesus; we want to know Your ways. Show us, teach us. Holy Spirit, we are hungry for the Kingdom of God.

CHAPTER 10

THE OIL OF THE SPIRIT

We talked previously about purity and power needing to exist together in our lives. Many times, the emphasis will be on being pure, but we don't realize that when we recognize something is powerful and make space for it around us, it demands higher standards of purity of motive to carry that weapon. When we shelve the power of God and the Holy Spirit, we devalue the need for purity. When we honor that God designed the Christian life to be one that can bring transformation, that the believer is called to be filled with His Spirit and cooperate with God and thus carries great power and authority, that belief demands that a believer be pure in motive and lifestyle. If my words are powerful then I must allow God to purify my heart, because it is from my heart that my mouth speaks. If my praise is a weapon in the hand of the Lord then bringing Him a pure sacrifice of praise matters. If the believer can bind things on earth and in Heaven, then surely the purity of my heart matters. We are in a season in which the Lord is once again emphasizing purity in the house of God because I believe He is wanting to demonstrate His mighty power in an incredible way. There is a stirring throughout the Body, an anticipation that something powerful is coming to the Church.

A year and a half after my encounter with the Holy Spirit, I was traveling from California to Colorado to speak at a conference. While I was in the San Francisco Airport, I was eating my lunch and reading an article on the Hebrides Revival. This revival happened in a small town in Scotland, initiated by the prayers of two older women in their 80s who were concerned about the status of the Church in their town. As I was reading about this incredible revival, I began sensing the presence of the Holy Spirit drawing close. He cannot help but draw near when we seek Him. All of a sudden (in the food court of the airport), I began to feel overwhelmed by Him.

Waves of the presence of God started to hit me, and immediately I knew it was significant. I could feel my mind start to sharpen as the Spirit of revelation Himself began to pull back the curtain of Heaven. I quickly took out my journal and began to write what I heard the Lord saying. The Holy Spirit began to prophesy over the coming season and what the Lord was about to do. I remember vigorously writing as God spoke to my heart about what He was determined to do. I wrote about a "remnant rising"—a people of God who had been called by Him, a people set apart because they had chosen to be.

As I wrote under the power of the Holy Spirit, the weight of His presence got heavier. Having experienced the powerful shaking I had just 18 months prior I knew all I needed to do was surrender to what He was doing. As I surrendered something started to shift, going from sharpness of mind to Him opening my eyes. I began to get caught up into Heaven, and He took me to the throne room. Unaware of where I now was physically, I began to encounter what I believe was a prophetic vision of this season.

Here is what I wrote:

> Time is starting again. I am starting the timer. I am flipping the order, I am flipping the order of authority. Old systems are getting turned in My favor. I am birthing a new order. The natural order is being shifted around.
>
> A new favor will rest on those who have surrendered to My fire—they carry My fire for reformation. There is a remnant rising; they have been tested in the fire.
>
> It's a 1 Corinthians 3:11-15 fire. That which was built unto another for "other" has been consumed, but what which now remains is Me. I am revealing Myself through sons and daughters who have yielded to My nature and likeness. Never before have you seen what I am about to do.
>
> The fire of Acts, of Azusa, will rest upon a company. With eyes like flint on My throne, they will march boldly, in unison, into the earth to reveal Me.
>
> I long to reveal My glory—time has started!
>
> You have been in a season of maturation, incubation, and birthing. I have asked for much and you

have willingly given. I am stepping in and coming through—for I am a covenant-keeping God and I never go back on My word. I kept my covenant with Abraham, with David, and with Hannah, and I will keep My covenant with you.

I have searched and I have found; a uniting of the church is coming. A three-cord strand is being woven.

I am birthing a fresh move in My apostles and prophets. They will be consumed with the heavenly mind and drawn to gaze, to gaze, to gaze. I am getting caught up right now, I'm gazing—the flashes of lightning on His robe are striking my heart and eyes. Attention and affection to be consumed with His beauty, majesty, and splendor. *All-powerful—all!* I see the host, I see the angels, I see them before Him, peaceful and powerful: "Worthy, worthy, worthy to receive all glory." There are golden bowls now; they look like they are being filled with oil that is coming from our worship. The oil in the bowls is living and it's moving and being poured one into another and spilling over. They are full of fragrance; it's the sound of the lover's song being poured out for Him.

There is something on His oil being poured out. The oil of Esther for preparation, the oil of David for anointing, the oil of Gilead for healing, the oil of Aaron for unity, and the oil of the 10 virgins for devotion to the Bridegroom. The Holy Spirit coming as oil to prepare for the fire.

I started to come out of this vision and realized that I had to make it to my gate for my flight—which proved to be quite tricky as I was still in a daze. During my flight, I feasted on an article about the Hebrides Revival and felt led after to read some of the book of Revelation. As I was reading from Revelation, I began to see the similarities between what was written there and what I had just experienced. It was truly amazing. While I was reflecting on what had happened, the Lord began to speak to me. He said, "Hayley, you love My fire, but I want to show you how I am oil." At first, I was unsure of what He meant. I know that a manifestation of the Holy Spirit is that He is like oil, but I did not really understand what that meant, but I was curious. I began asking the Lord questions and looking through stories in the Bible that spoke of the oil of the Lord.

THE SPIRIT LIKE OIL

In the Old Covenant, the Holy Spirit had not been released on all flesh as they were waiting for what was prophesied for the coming "last days" in Joel 2:28. From the very beginning, the Spirit has been brooding and breathing as the Father declared life over creation. As the Lord would raise up men and women in the Old Covenant, He would release His Spirit upon them for specific assignments. When the Lord would call a man or woman to a task, He would instruct them to be anointed with oil for the assignment. The priests were those initially anointed with oil, and later kings and prophets. The anointing of oil was an act to set apart the individual or object as holy and sanctify them for the work of service to the Lord. In 1 Samuel 16:13, David the shepherd boy was anointed with oil to be king, and when he was the Spirit of God came upon him in power and remained with him from that day forward. The oil was the sign of something or, better yet, Someone far more powerful than simply the liquid poured—it was the sign of God's Spirit.

The "anointing" is not a sign of someone's spirituality but rather the evidence of the Person of the Spirit resting on the individual's life. The gifts of the Spirit are not meant to point to someone's great spiritual prowess but instead create in them a deep hunger for and dependence on the Spirit of God. The name of the Spirit of God is the "Holy Spirit" or the "Holy Ghost," and that is because He is holy in every way. He is completely perfect in His ways, and just like the oil of anointing in the Old Covenant signified the sanctification and setting apart of the person being anointed, so does the coming of the Spirit signify the same upon us in the New Covenant. There is a powerful declaration from Heaven over us in this season, and it is one of being set apart and made holy like He is holy. God is looking for a pure and devoted Bride. This can only be done by the work of the Holy Spirit in our lives. We must welcome His oil to be poured out upon us and do a work in us, to purify us, and set us apart. To address any thought or deed that is not of Him and remove it, to ready us for His holy fire. This is His work and our surrender.

And He, when He comes, will convict the world regarding sin, and righteousness, and judgment (John 16:8 NASB).

HIS OIL OF PREPARATION

The Lord then took me to the story of Esther in her season before she met the king. Esther was taken through a series of beauty treatments, which included being bathed in oil for a year. The story of Esther was powerful then, for the sake of her people, but it also speaks prophetically of the Bride of Christ who is being readied to meet her Bridegroom, Jesus. Oh, what a glorious day that will be when we meet Jesus face to face.

The oil for the beauty treatments Esther received existed to cleanse these virgins from the effects of the previous season and infuse them with a new fragrance. The first six months of treatment would be bathing in oil to remove dirt, smell, and damage from the elements (sun/wind) in the previous season. The next six months would be bathing in oil for beautifying, and that was infused with beautiful fragrance. These young women would not only receive cleansing from the harshness of the last season, but a new fragrance would now permeate their skin and they would smell like this new oil. This oil would change the complexion of the bride and the fragrance of the last season would be replaced with a sweet, pleasant aroma.

As I was reading and pondering, the Lord began to draw the parallel between this oil and what the oil of the Holy Spirit was being poured out for in this season. The Covid-19 outbreak was brutal for humankind. It was surely a season we all needed to be cleansed from and the Lord knew it, and He was coming through for us. Not only does the Holy Spirit set us apart and convict us, but He cleanses us from contamination. He comes as oil to heal us from past hurt, rejection, trauma, pain—the list could go on and on. And He does not just cleanse us and heal us from this, but He takes that which was meant for our destruction and transforms it for our good.

I wondered how many times have I cried out for fire to burn away chaff, but what we actually needed was for His oil to gently cleanse us and transform us? I love the fire of God and how He purifies us in that fire, but here the Holy Spirit was showing me a tenderness in Him that I had not known before. He was showing me that in this season of struggle, though He loves being the fire, He was meeting us where we needed, and we needed tender care. He wasn't in a rush but was so willing to sit with us and soak us in His presence. All of us have experienced seasons of challenge and pain. We all know the effects of hardship and how they can linger with us beyond the season. My encounter with the Holy Spirit did not only unveil the lies I was believing and their awful effects on my life lived thus far but completely crushed them by His coming. He dealt with things I thought I would live with for the rest of my existence and showed me His victory. He took my eyes off the attack of the enemy and put them on the Wonderful Counselor and Almighty God who was for me. He replaced the lies with the reality of His goodness and His presence with me. When the enemy tries to come in and disrupt, God does not only come to crush the enemy's plan, but the Lord responds to us by giving of Himself in greater measure.

A little while ago my daughter needed to have a procedure on her ears and had to be put under anesthesia. To monitor her vitals while she was under, they stuck these monitors on her chest. Now, I do not understand why those loving doctors sent her home with those blessed things stuck on her chest but they did. (I'm sure they had a great reason.) They gave us some little alcohol pads to run under the corners to help remove them. Well, the first attempt to lift a little corner and rub that little alcohol swab under was a complete disaster. My girl felt the first tug on her skin and lost it. She was screaming, fighting, and would not let us near those things. We tried the next best thing we could think of—maybe if we put her in the bath they would soak off? The minute she saw the pads on her chest she freaked out again and just wanted her shirt back on. I was at a loss. I couldn't leave these pads on her chest indefinitely, but she seemed traumatized and I felt completely helpless.

All of a sudden a thought came to me, "What if I get something oily on there?" I went and got some oil-based cream and in a couple of swipes, in between some screams, I rubbed oil around those little patches. Thirty minutes later I came back to them and got more oil on and under them. Each time I returned, more of the patch had come off, and the oil continued to loosen them without the same pain as before. Eventually, where the patches had been completely stuck, now they slid off her chest.

This is what happens when we allow ourselves to be continually saturated by the Holy Spirit. Things that have been stuck to us for decades that we have thought are impossible to heal from or see removed from our lives, after time saturated in Him, seem to slide off with ease. Shame that hounded us loses its grip in an encounter with the Holy Spirit.

HIS OIL TO TRANSFORM

One of my greatest issues with the "self-help" industry is this belief that it is all on me because "no one is going to help me unless I help myself." What we don't realize is that this is godless thinking. Or to say it another way, it is thinking without Jesus at the center of my story. The thought that I have to rely on myself alone to get through my struggles or pain is completely negating the work of Christ. This is not the Gospel; it is a lie. The world is peddling a message of self-dependence and reliance that has built its house on the sand of human wisdom, and it cannot withstand the storm. I believe through poor biblical literacy and understanding of who God is, we have reduced faith to our own understanding.

We feel the lack in our own lives, the gaps where we are not sufficient, and we have tried to fill them with more knowledge when what we need is more knowledge of who God is. The truth is that we don't need to close the gaps in our lives; we need to surrender every one of them to the Lord. God has made provision to close every gap in our lives with His very presence. I am not saying that we don't have a responsibility in this—of course, we do. Our responsibility is to bring ourselves before the Lord and withhold nothing from Him. To partner with His leading and follow in obedience. The effort we put in is not in our strength but in reliance on His strength. A life of dependence on the Lord is not lazy; it is engaged and purposeful in every step. Eyes, ears, and hearts fully attentive to His leading, yielded in humility to our need for Him. The Holy Spirit is our Helper and our Comforter, and He comes like oil to heal our wounds, restore our brokenness, and transform us into the likeness of Jesus.

HE LACKS NOTHING

The Spirit is coming like oil to prepare the Bride to meet Jesus our Bridegroom.

> *The Law came in so that the offense would increase; but where sin increased, grace abounded all the more, so that, as sin reigned in death, so also grace would reign through righteousness to eternal life through Jesus Christ our Lord* (Romans 5:20-21 NASB).

This passage tells us that no matter how much the enemy tries to affect us, no matter how much sin exists in or around us, the availability of God's grace will increase beyond the plans of the evil one. Where the enemy rises against us, He meets us with more of His presence as the solution every time. God does not simply want to end the war in our lives, He wants to heal and restore us to live a life of abundance. This is why He is oil. God doesn't simply hand us a tool to overcome hardship, He pours Himself out upon us.

In the Bible times the shepherds would pour oil on the heads of their sheep to keep pests and parasites away from bothering them and laying eggs in their ears, eyes, or nose. You could imagine the distraction that it would pose for the sheep to have an insect do this. Our good Shepherd anoints us with His Spirit like oil to bring relief and deliverance from the distracting, exhausting, and overwhelming attack of the enemy (see Psalm 23:5). The Person of the Holy Spirit, available to us as oil so that we can be cleansed, restored, and run our race with longevity but also joy. First, the oil exists to cleanse, protect and restore, but it goes beyond that—it transforms us and makes us glad.

HIS OIL SUSTAINS HIS FIRE

Fire without oil is like striking a match—it's a big flash but has no longevity. The Holy Spirit was speaking to my heart of how I have seen some powerful "explosive" moments, but He wants us to know Him as oil so that we may continually carry a holy fire. Encounters with the Lord are not supposed to just be moments of experience but doors of invitation to know Him more. The Holy Spirit wants us to know Him as the Sustainer so that the

Church would carry a raging fire of His presence. Reinhard Bonnke once said at a graduation our school was hosting, "Flies cannot sit on a hot stove." The oil of intimacy allows our fire of passion and love for the Lord to burn hot and vigorously so that no lie of the enemy could rest on us for too long.

Matthew 25:1-13 tells quite a challenging story of ten virgins—a story in which there were five foolish maidens who did not keep the oil in their lamps full and five wise maidens who did. When the time came for the groom to return, those with oil were able to attend the wedding banquet, but those without were locked out. The focus for us should be on the five wise women, for this is the heart of God for us—that we would enter the Marriage Supper of the Lamb. We need the oil of intimacy flowing in our lives if we are to sustain the fire of love for our King. We get this oil through our daily devotion to the Lord. These are not often grand moments or ones that anyone would write books about, but instead the oil of love is gathered in deep devotion. Intimacy is not cultivated through a simple moment, but it is the presence of many moments of attentiveness, care, and investment that are strung together to form a bond that can withstand the storm.

To live a life of devotion to the Lord is far greater than any accolade the world could bestow on us. Devotion and obedience is the greatest desire of His heart over sacrifice and success. A life of intimacy is one that lives every moment with the Groom in mind, and this life will produce the fruit of connection. You cannot sit at His feet as Mary did and not get full of vision to serve what is in His heart. To buy oil requires faith in His coming; this faith gives us attentiveness to a King who is preparing us now. To buy oil is costly to our dignity and understanding at times. It means we prize His voice and heart over everything else. A life with oil is one in which the flame of love is always lit and His fire remains burning brightly. As we look to Him and are attentive to our relationship with Jesus, the Holy Spirit fills our lamps with His oil and we overflow with His love.

HIS OIL ON LIVING STONES

And he happened upon a particular place and spent the night there, because the sun had set; and he took one of the stones of the place and made it a support for his head, and lay down in that place. And he had a dream, and behold, a ladder was set up on the earth with its top reaching to heaven; and behold, the angels of God were ascending and descending on it. Then behold, the Lord was standing above it and said, "I am the Lord, the God of your father Abraham and the God of Isaac; the land on which you lie I will give to you and to your descendants. Your descendants will also be like the dust of the earth, and you will spread out to the west and to the east, and to the north and to the south; and in you and in your descendants shall all the families of the earth be blessed. Behold, I am with you and will keep you wherever you go, and will bring you back to this land; for I will not leave you until I have done what I have promised you." Then Jacob awoke from his sleep and said, "The Lord is certainly in this place, and I did not know it!" And he was afraid and said, "How awesome is this place! This is none other than the house of God, and this is the gate of heaven!"

So Jacob got up early in the morning, and took the stone that he had placed as a support for his head, and set it up as a memorial stone, and poured oil on its top. Then he named that place Bethel; but previously the name of the city had been Luz (Genesis 28:11-19 NASB).

In this story, Jacob has fled from his brother and is alone in the wilderness. It grows dark and he needs a place to sleep, so he sets up a rock as a pillow. Once he falls asleep, he has a heavenly dream about a ladder coming from Heaven and connecting to earth with angels ascending and descending on it. Once he wakes up, he comes to the understanding that he is in a holy place and declares that it is the "house of God, the gate of Heaven." In his response to this revelation, he pours oil out on the rock that he had used as a pillow and renames the place *Bethel* (house of God).

This is an incredible prophetic revelation that we are standing in. In the natural, Jacob is anointing a rock, but in the spirit he is prophesying something to come. In 1 Peter 2:5 (NASB), we are called living stones.

You also, as living stones, are being built up as a spiritual house for a holy priesthood, to offer up spiritual sacrifices that are acceptable to God through Jesus Christ.

Just as Jacob poured oil on the rock, so the outpouring of the Holy Spirit on the Church as living stones has made us the house of God and a gate of Heaven. What is a gate? A gate connects one thing to another. For example, my back yard to my front yard has a gate in between, and the only way to access my back yard from my front yard is to go through the gate. When the oil of the Holy Spirit is poured out on His people and we encounter Him for who He is, we become ambassadors of Heaven. Jesus said, "Greater works will you do in My name." In the name of Jesus, we as the people of God carry His precious Holy Spirit, which means we have the authority and access to the power of the resurrected Christ in us. Our mandate is to drive back the darkness by revealing a greater Kingdom, the Kingdom of God. We do this as Jesus did, empowered by the Holy Spirit.

The baptism of the Holy Spirit and the stewardship of His presence within us enables us to live the life Jesus calls us to live. Every encounter is deeply personal and cannot be compared because God is doing a work that is unique to our makeup and mandate. Each of us has been designed with a purpose, and as we live in our God-given purpose we fit together perfectly. When we understand just how personal God is toward us, that He would fill our very beings with His Spirit, we realize that comparison is pointless because we are embraced by Him in our uniqueness. Encounters are not supposed to be a competition in the body of Christ but instead a personal revelation of our need for His work in us. Just as the disciples competed around Jesus, so at times we can get competitive with one another. This isn't a spiritual contest; instead, it is for each of us to grow in awareness of how much we need the Lord in our respective lives to become the fullness of His design and desire.

THE OIL OF THE HOLY SPIRIT BRINGS UNITY

We mentioned this before but in the context of this chapter I want to make note of the unity that is coming because I believe we are about to see a uniting of the Church in a way that we have not seen since its inception. Psalm 133:1-3 talks about the unity of the children of God like oil dripping down the beard of Aaron, the first high priest. The anointing of the Spirit of God and unity of the Bride go hand in hand. The Church in Acts experienced an incredible unity when the outpouring of the Spirit came upon them. They were not unified around agreement but were unified under one Spirit and one King. The work of the Holy Spirit in our lives produces the fruit we need to live in unity, not uniformity. Uniformity is sameness, but unity is oneness.

Throughout Paul's writings, he is clear in sharing about the different gifts that each of us possess as the body of Christ. Not one of us is a complete individual on our own but each of us a member of each other (see Romans 12:5). We all possess different gifts and abilities; when brought together, we form the body of Christ. In 1 Corinthians 12, Paul teaches about the gifts of the Spirit in their many forms. In 1 Corinthians 14, Paul talks about the gift of prophecy for the building up and edification of the church. Paul seems to pause by writing about love in 1 Corinthians 13—or does he? I don't believe this passage about love is a pause, but it is, in fact, a reminder of the purpose of the gifts of the Spirit. The church of Corinth was highly spiritual and were showing of their gifts to esteem themselves in their spirituality. Imagine them walking around speaking in tongues to show spiritual prowess; and while others were amazed, no one was understanding what was being said. In this passage they are being reminded that the prime purpose for spiritual gifts is not to puff ourselves up but to build up one another in love.

There is much beauty in realizing we as individuals are the temple of the Holy Spirit. But our own salvation and infilling of the Spirit is unto something even greater—that the earth may recognize Jesus in us and be filled with His glory. God desires that none should perish but that all would know Jesus as Redeemer and King. It is when we come together under one head, Christ Jesus, and in the power of His Spirit, the Holy Spirit, that the Church walks in her true identity—His body.

> *As you come to him, the living Stone—rejected by humans but chosen by God and precious to him—you also, like living stones, are being built into a spiritual house to be a holy priesthood, offering spiritual sacrifices acceptable to God through Jesus Christ* (1 Peter 2:4-5 NIV).

This passage takes us from individual temples to being stones fit together as one temple to host Him. We belong to each other because we belong to Jesus.

> *For through him we both have access in one Spirit to the Father. So then you are no longer strangers and aliens, but you are fellow citizens with the saints and members of the household of God, built on the foundation of the apostles and prophets, Christ Jesus himself being the cornerstone, in whom the whole structure, being joined together, grows into a holy temple in the Lord. In him you also are being built together into a dwelling place for God by the Spirit* (Ephesians 2:18-22 ESV).

There has been immense discord and factions in the body. It is heartbreaking to see the willingness of believers to disconnect and disrespect one another publicly, speaking ill of other denominations or streams. The Spirit does not give gifts to elevate or divide but to build one another up and for us all to enter into the truth that without dependence on Him we truly do not have anything. Jesus is responding and inviting us into a deep dependence on Him. This dependence on Him keeps us aware that we have all received this precious gift by mercy, and not one of us could do it on our own. We need an outpouring of the Spirit on the Bride so that we might walk in the love of God for one another and unity together as His body. The Spirit enables us to forgive, to let go of offense, and to remain humble. Humility comes from our proximity to the Lord, meaning the closer we get to Him the smaller we realize we are. Humility isn't us making ourselves small but more realizing how big Jesus is and how much we need Him. God in His love is responding to us and bringing adjustment where we need it most.

The oil of the Spirit is coming to prepare us. He is coming to remove the effect of hardship and trauma, to remove labels and lies, to fill us with His fragrance, to anoint us to bring Heaven to earth, and to unify His Bride. I believe we are going to see a unifying of the streams of God in a way we have not seen before. The Lord is braiding us together by the power of His Spirit. May we yield to this outpouring of His oil, for our God is an all-consuming fire, and the fire must never go out.

> Holy Spirit, pour Yourself like oil out upon us. Heal us, restore us, forgive us, and bind us together in Your love. Spirit of the living God, come and fall afresh on us. Remove any effects of the last season and ready us for Your holy fire. We are hungry for a fresh outpouring, Holy Spirit, send revival to our land so that we might walk as one body, under one head, glorifying our precious Lord, Jesus Christ.

CHAPTER 11

A REFORMATION

TIMES AND SEASONS

I wanted to take this last chapter to talk about something I have been sensing prophetically that the Holy Spirit is emphasizing for us in this season. First Chronicles 12:32 talks about the sons of Issachar, who understood the times and what Israel should do. These men walked in a godly understanding of the moment they found themselves in and the wisdom to apply action to that understanding of the circumstances. Walking closely with the Holy Spirit allows us to intimately engage with the thoughts and ways of God and partner with what He is doing. Isaiah 11 speaks of various functions of the Holy Spirit, one of which is the *"spirit of wisdom and understanding"* in verse 2. Because this is one of the functions of the Spirit and we have Him dwelling in us, we can rest assured knowing we can rely on the Spirit to reveal to us the seasons we are walking in and what to do in these seasons to partner with the Lord in them.

Have you ever been in a season when you can feel things are changing, but you can't see any evidence of it in the natural? I often feel like I live in this space, and recently within this tension my heart has been so stirred for the Bride of Christ. I have been crying out to God for this fresh move of His Spirit that I sense He is longing to pour out on His people. In this prayer time, I started to feel antsy, like I just wanted things to "hurry up." Praying for God to hasten is a legal prayer. We see it in the Psalms as David cries out for help. This prayer is not because God is slow or unaware but because, by His mercy, He has chosen a partnership with us; we are called His friends, and so He can be moved by our prayers and bring acceleration. Prayer is more for us than for Him; we need a prayer life because it anchors us in the God-life.

However, my prayer to hasten in this season was more impatience than hunger at that point. I thought I knew what needed to happen and was getting stuck in the outcome. God's response to me was quick and to the point. He told me, "Hayley, recognize the moment you are in." His words hit my heart and mind; it was like I could suddenly see clearly, and what I saw gave me great faith. He gave me wisdom and revelation in this moment. God doesn't scorn or ignore our cries in frustration. He is a good Father, and He inclines His ear and brings us the truth we need in order to walk in the hope of His calling. Truth can be sharp, but when it is truly said in love it cuts off hindrances and weight and liberates us to run the race that has been set before us.

The minute God spoke, life and vision entered my being, and I saw that we were already in the beginnings of the outpouring—it was just in infancy, like a little shoot coming out of the ground after the acorn had been planted. That little shoot is already an oak tree, it just needs someone to recognize it in its infancy, nurture it, and protect it, and it can become all that it is destined to become. We as humans are not often ones to enjoy the process. We try to bypass it and look to the outcome as a sign of success, but that thinking fails to recognize the value of what is being built. The wineskin is necessary for the wine. God is building something in His Church and doing it unto a tremendous outpouring of His Spirit so that we might know the Lord and see Him rightly. To see Jesus rightly, we must embrace the work of His Spirit in our lives and the body so that we might know Him and follow His ways entirely.

WE ARE IN A REFORMATION

We are in both a wonderful and challenging season because we, in this generation, are in a massive reformation season. Much of what society has believed and embraced as moral truth is being questioned and challenged. We are questioning everything that pertains to our identity, from our sexuality and gender to the nuclear family structure. There is contention over when human life begins, putting ourselves in the place of God rather than being led by Him. In the name of freedom, we have forgotten that we are also responsible, and every choice and decision we make now will have a consequence, good or bad. This reformation is not simply one for the Church but one attempting to reform the Church itself, and it will affect the foundation of all people. It is a reformation of thought and the principles by which we will live our lives. Pillars that have formed society, like "love" and "truth," are being challenged, and people are attempting to change their definitions. Eternal, godly values are being questioned, and attempts have been made to have them adjusted to fit our finite human understanding and comfort level. Thus, we are seeing a breakdown in the fabric of humankind. How could this be wonderful, you ask? Well, if we are in a reformation that is not yet complete, then we get to engage and decide—will culture reform us, or will we let Jesus reform us?

I believe we are in a battle for land promised to God's people, and the enemy would love to occupy it. The many fundamental areas of a healthy society are being contended for to redefine how we should live and what we should believe. Just like Joshua and Caleb, the Lord is showing us the land He has given us, but we must have eyes to see what He is doing and not the size of the giants threatening us. The Bride of Christ must be awakened by His Spirit to His great victory and a renewed faith in the power of Jesus and His authority to carry it forth.

WE ARE CREATED BEINGS

What is so fascinating about this reformation is that we believe as human beings that we could somehow redefine something we didn't make or create. Of course, we can change laws and alter our lives, but the fruit of living outside of the Maker's intention is unhealthy and leads to bondage. We have been designed, fashioned, and created by God. We did not make ourselves nor design this world. When society forsakes its Creator and King and worships creation itself (see Romans 1:25), we begin to see the degradation of the true moral (biblical) fabric and vision and hope destroyed in our midst. Everything God created is incredibly intricate and intentional, and He has created a structure for it to thrive. We can throw the whole system off when we adjust small parts of this complex design. A small amount of yeast will affect all the dough, a small about of poison affects the whole stream, and embracing "small" lies affects all of society.

In this reformation, either the Church can be reformed by the thoughts and beliefs of the world or we can partner with the Lord. We must allow Him to transform us and join in His reformation, which invites the redeemed into a partnership to bring His transformation to the world.

> *In those days there was no king in Israel. Everyone did what was right in his own eyes* (Judges 21:25).

This passage rocks me every time I revisit it. First, it is one that reveals where humanity ends up when they do not have King Jesus ruling and reigning. When Jesus is not on the throne of our hearts, we are ruled by confusing and contradicting standards that no one can define. We lose our moral compass and live unrestrained and thus without vision or purpose, giving in to the demand of our flesh instead of yielding to our Creator God and His will (see Proverbs 29:18).

This passage in Judges brings me both comfort and holy fear. On one hand, I am comforted because it reminds me that this is not the first time humankind has faced what we are experiencing, and therefore God has a plan and strategy to bring salvation to our current state. We are not alone, nor are we powerless, because God is with us and moving on our behalf. And while I hope, I am also provoked by this reformation to a place where I realize we cannot do this alone. We must seek the Lord, anchor ourselves in His truth, and learn from those who have gone before us to build a better future for our children and their children.

This passage brings me to holy fear because it reminds me that it is not good and never has been good for us to lead ourselves in complete autonomy. I am not designed to live in dependence on my own thoughts and understanding but in dependence on Jesus and the power of His Spirit and in connection with His body. Judges is a book in which we clearly see the effects of humankind trying to lead themselves and the breakdown of the moral fabric of society when they do.

We weren't created to lead ourselves because we didn't make ourselves. Our role is to steward what God has given us under His leadership. You didn't design one part of your makeup—God designed you. Every need, personality trait, and function of your physical body was purposefully designed and created to function in full connection with your God and submission to His ways. Every truth is fundamental to His design and has a purpose and a way it must operate to thrive. Sure, there are unconventional ways we can use what we have been given, some

A REFORMATION

with greater consequences than others, and just because it has worked once doesn't mean it's safe or healthy.

When we discard the manual and live only by feeling or experience, we are playing in the danger zone, and at some point someone will get very hurt. For example, if you went to the hairdresser and suddenly your stylist came out of the back carrying a chainsaw, you would probably start questioning whether or not you would stay for your scheduled appointment. Maybe your stylist would tell you of the last client and how fabulous it looked or how great they felt, but this still does not mean that it is a safe or proper use. Even if it has been done before does not mean that it should be done again.

When we disconnect from the heart of our Creator and God's "why" behind His design, we take a seat on the throne of our lives and start making judgments on "the truth" that is unhealthy at best and at worst completely destructive.

GOD RAISES UP THE REFORMERS

The book of 1 Samuel is chronologically after the book of Judges ends. Eli and Samuel were the final judges of Israel, and Samuel was the one who anointed the first king. First Samuel 2:12-36 tells the story of Eli's sons and the abomination they were to the priesthood. In the Old Covenant, the priests were the only ones allowed in the presence of God—it was a privilege. God called priests to minister to Him and serve the people of God so the people may be connected to God. But Eli's sons had no regard for the law of God, nor for the purity with which they were called to live, and they lived selfishly and as they pleased. These were dark days that people were living because they were living according to their own truth and not God's.

Right in the midst of all this darkness, God makes a declaration that is about to change everything. God has a plan for humanity and He states it in 1 Samuel 2:35 (NASB):

But I will raise up for Myself a faithful priest who will do according to what is in My heart and My soul; and I will build him an enduring house, and he will walk before My anointed always.

God in His mercy and wisdom chose to raise up a priest and a prophet who will seek after Him and Him alone. A young boy who will devote his life to seeking the face of God and ministering in His house and to the heart of God. The life of Samuel is one to be studied in this season. Samuel carried an understanding and devotion that was paramount to the shift that needed to come to the house of Israel, and the Lord is inviting us into this same devotion.

GOODNESS AND HOLINESS

This devotion of Samuel's life we are talking about is not just one of friendship but a devotion that has established God's lordship in every aspect of it.

In the last season, we saw many leaders preach and teach with a powerful understanding of the nature of God being good. This message was a much-needed revelation that broke through legalism and stoic religion that we as the Church needed in order to enter into right understanding of who the Father is and His freedom. As many leaders in the faith began to unpack the nature of God being good and His heart toward us, the Church awoke and the Gospel spread far and wide. We saw the great Jesus Movement being birthed, and the Church began to walk in the grace and mercy of the cross as many unsaved came to know Jesus as Savior and Lord. We have lived in the abundant fruit of this move, and it has been paramount for us to understand the beauty of God's grace and thus the advancement of His Kingdom over the last several decades. God has been establishing in His Bride that He is good, His kindness endures forever, and His mercy toward us is new every morning. This is a foundation that must not be moved. His goodness is foundational to us surrendering our lives to Him as a living sacrifice. Romans 12:1 clearly states that it is in viewing God's mercy that we offer ourselves to Him. It is not logical to give ourselves to the One who is called "an all-consuming fire" unless that fire is for us and consumes that which hinders and causes us great harm.

The challenge we find for ourselves in this season, however, is that as the world increases the message of self-service and self-lordship, we need the revelation of a good God who does not get filtered through "self" but is held in the full picture of all God is. Our God calls Himself our friend, but He is still Lord and King. He calls Himself good and kind, but He is also holy. As people assimilate the revelation of His magnificent goodness, we face the challenge of attributing His goodness to a worldly definition of "goodness," which is centered on "my preference" and not His nature. We may not filter the Lord's nature through our lens of understanding and begin to draw conclusions about what He is like. It is by His holy Word that we define and know our King. His greatness and omnipotence do not fit through our finite understanding, and we must not and cannot discard one part of His nature in order to embrace another. We must rather hold the tension of what He says about Himself and allow it to do a great work in us—this will keep us rightly related to Him. A message that does not carry God's holiness and over-emphasizes the comfort of His nature will produce irreverence in the hearts of the believers, giving them the license to pick and choose what part of the Lord they want to follow. But this is impossible and destructive.

The privilege of our friendship with Jesus only comes when we have submitted to His lordship—we can only go deep in friendship with Jesus to the degree we are willing to submit to His lordship. The absolutely obedient heart is the heart that Jesus reveals His mysteries to. A life completely yielded to Him is the only way to begin to know His fullness. As we have entered into and enjoyed the freedom God's goodness brings, we must also grasp that He is utterly holy and set apart from all sin. While in His mercy and kindness we are free to make choices in any and every moment of our lives, if we are to walk in His ways and carry His authority we must completely submit to His lordship and embrace His holiness. We simply cannot carry His authority if we are not under it.

The goodness and awe of God speak of a holy God who paid the highest price so that we might enter into union with Him without separation or distance from Him. His holiness is entirely separate from any compromise and terrifyingly pure. Holiness is completely impossible for us to connect to because of our sin. This union can only be entered into one way, the way God established, which is through the cross of Jesus where we are covered and washed in His blood. There is no other way to live in connection with God except by the sacrifice of His Son, and that requires us to be obedient to His way.

A theology that is void of the fear of the Lord lacks power and the need for us to walk in holiness. If God is not a raging fire of holiness, then our sin has nothing to stand against it. If God is not a roaring lion, then our enemy has no reason to be afraid. Isaiah 11:3 says that Jesus delighted in the fear of the Lord. He took delight in the awe, wonder, and absolutely terrifying greatness of God. Jesus walked in a reverence that we must grasp to know our Lord and walk in His ways.

How can we delight in the fear of the Lord? Because we have received His mercy. His great mercy that is new each day allows us to enter a holy place no man could on their own (see Lamentations 3:23). By the blood of the spotless Lamb of God that was spilled for our freedom and wholeness, we receive God's mercy. His mercy must not be taken for granted; it must be revered. When God's goodness and the fear of the Lord are embraced in the heart of the believer, entitlement bows, and deep gratitude and joyful praise of our King abounds. The life lived in awe and gratitude toward God is the life lived in incessant joy and the abundance of Jesus. To live under His lordship is to live truly liberated. His leadership is perfect in every way, and we need it to live the life promised in John 10:10.

THE PRIEST AND THE PROPHETIC CALL

We are in an exciting time, when the Holy Spirit is pouring Himself out upon us so that we might know God in a deeper and more powerful way. This is a time when we as the church will embrace the nature of God even in the face of trial. Trials strengthen our resolve, and God will use these challenges we face to strengthen our resolve of who He is and what He does. In the midst of great confusion, I see the Lord ushering in a holy reverence and awe upon His Bride. Where the fear of man overplays its hand, the Lord will usher in the Spirit of the fear of the Lord.

In this holy reverence for who He is, we will become acutely aware of any place we have tried to add or subtract from it, and the Church will come into repentance and a newfound freedom in Christ. We are alive for such a time as this. There is a sobering coming to the Bride as she realizes she is His chosen dwelling, His royal priesthood, and a holy nation. For us to stand in the truth of who God is we need to walk in the ways of the Spirit and have the awareness of our hunger and need for the work of the Holy Spirit in us to constantly increase.

> For to us God revealed them through the Spirit; for the Spirit searches all things, even the depths of God. For who among people knows the thoughts of a person except the spirit of the person that is in him? So also the thoughts of God no one knows, except the Spirit of God. Now we have not received the spirit of the world, but the Spirit who is from God, so that we may know the things freely given to us by God. We also speak these things, not in words taught by human wisdom, but in those taught by the Spirit, combining spiritual thoughts with spiritual words.

> But a natural person does not accept the things of the Spirit of God, for they are foolishness to him; and he cannot understand them, because they are spiritually discerned. But the one who is spiritual discerns all things, yet he himself is discerned by no one. For who has known the mind of the Lord, that he will instruct Him? But we have the mind of Christ (1 Corinthians 2:10-16 NASB).

I believe the Lord's response to our need in this season is to raise up priests and prophetic voices in our midst who will reveal His heart in purity and truth and draw the people of God into the same. Just as God raised up Samuel, David, Elijah, and John the Baptist, so He is raising up His priests and prophets to bring a cry that will usher us into this Holy Reformation. The beauty of this is that each of these mighty ones raised up by the Lord were ordinary people who gave themselves completely to Him. Oftentimes we see the words "priests" or "prophets" and we discount ourselves, but the eyes of the Lord are looking for faithful and often ordinary ones whom He can trust to place His Spirit on in a marked way.

God's solution in times of cultural reformation is to first bring a personal reformation of those called to minister to Him and to His people. The ministers to God's heart and from His heart must be calibrated to what is burning within Him so that the Bride of Christ will walk in step with Heaven. Because of this, we are seeing a holy move of God coming to the worship and the prophetic movement because they are those ministries that minister to and from His heart. The Holy Spirit is coming like oil and fire to purify those who walk in these callings so the Church may walk in purity and in the power of the Holy Spirit. He is cleansing our lenses and our hearts so that we will behold the Lamb of God and represent Jesus rightly. The Lord is bringing purity and reformation to our worship as the people of God. He is building us stronger than ever so that we might see Him rightly and clearly.

OUR WORSHIP AS THE BRIDE

The prayer and worship movement is being raised up in the Body with great power and authority. This generation is growing up with instant fixes, pseudo connections, and an abundance of all kinds of information, more than any generation has ever experienced. The Lord is responding by inviting us to know true authority to bring Kingdom solutions. Prayer is one of the greatest spiritual practices we can participate in as it does more for us than anything else. Prayer shapes us, teaches, and molds in us the heart of God and His character. The act of prayer, when done the way Jesus taught, is one of partnership with the Holy Spirit, in deep connection with the will of the Father, walking in the victory Jesus has given us. True prayer and intercession are not convincing God of what we want, but it is to sit before the throne of God and hear what is on His heart and release it by the authority we have in Jesus's name. Intercession is not something to simply do by practice but by a partnership with the Holy Spirit and His moving on the earth.

To be people of prayer, we will have to walk in the Spirit and not in the flesh. One of the antidotes to the fast-paced, production-based society we live in is to commit to a life of prayer so that we might walk in His ways and at His pace. Prayer will cause us to become aware of and invested in a Kingdom we do not see with eyes of flesh but with eyes open to a realm greater than the one we see. It is the eyes of the heart that must be awakened by the Holy Spirit, like the eyes of the servant of Elisha in 2 Kings 6 that we looked at in Chapter 7 on faith. The Holy

Spirit is inviting us to yield to His ways so that our eyes would be spiritually opened to see the Kingdom and form us into the likeness of the King.

CLEANSING OUR LENSES IN REPENTANCE

I recently sat under a powerful teaching from a man named Corey Russell, on the gift of tears and how it brings clarity to our lenses. I am not sure that I had thought of tears as a gift prior to my encounter, but from my personal experience I have now come to love when God moves me to tears because of what it did for my heart. Crying for many can feel embarrassing, but to the Lord our tears before Him are offerings of love and the demonstration of a heart that is soft to Him. When the Holy Spirit comes like oil, He is preparing the Bride for a holy fire that is to come. The tears we will cry in His presence will be used to clean the lenses of the eyes of our hearts so that any obstruction or skewed perspective will be removed.

The cleansing of the lenses to behold the Lamb can only happen in repentance. I know we talked about repentance earlier, but I wanted to reiterate that *"the kindness of God leads you to repentance"* (Romans 2:4 NASB). Repentance isn't shaming—it is liberating. As we see His holiness, we will see our deep need for Him to purify us. The Holy Spirit is coming to convict us to return to our first love and those early days of awakening to our need for His presence to be with us. I can feel it stirring in the Bride right now. The tears of first love and repentance are coming like a wave of remembrance. Places where our hearts have been hardened or become apathetic are being pressed on by the hand of the Lord to remind us of what it feels like to be alive in Him. It is only in Him that we *"live and move and have our being"* (Acts 17:28 ESV). And just like that Acts 17 moment when Paul walks amongst the gods of Athens and introduces them to the one true living God, so the Spirit moves among all the idols that we have lined up in our lives. In power, He is proclaiming there is only one King, one Lord, and His name is Jesus.

The refining of our solutions and strategies is coming, and it is boiling down to one thing—the King and His Kingdom. Jesus is the only redemption, the only salvation, the only solution, and He is more than sufficient. Just like in David's generation, the priests called to lead and minister in this generation are being awakened to their desire and need for the Lord. Some right now are wandering in the wilderness of their soul. They have found great fame, and yet the applause of man did not satisfy. Their hearts have become dull from the complexity that "ministry" became, and they are being wooed back to first love. There is a move of the Spirit that is coming to our worshipers and ministers that is going to be so profound and holy that we don't even have the words to explain it. The lost ones are being pulled in, the jaded are being shaken up, and the Lord is restoring the ministry of His heart to His priests. The work of the Holy Spirit is already in action in the hearts of these ones. Some are already feeling His wooing, and they are responding.

I want to be honest, though, I don't see this simply being light and quick. I believe it will carry immense weight for those willing to bear it and, at times, deep grief as we feel the ache in God's heart. I do not believe we will steward this outpouring of God's heart without deep and vulnerable repentance. This repentance will not come by a man-made mandate but by a sobering move of the Spirit in our midst. Oh, the beauty of repentance before the Lord that we will know and come to embrace. This alignment the Lord is bringing will come with a weighty glory that will press on and shake that which is shakable but only to establish that which is eternal. Altars built in our hearts to other gods are going to be torn down in the move of His holiness, and it won't take but a moment in the resting of His glorious presence. The weight of His glory that leads to repentance will lead to us being able to behold the beauty of His glory that He is revealing. The weeping of repentance will be a sweet liberation of His priests and will wash the debris that clouds their view of their lenses so we can see Jesus rightly. Any offense, disappointment, or disillusionment is being washed away in the sweetness and glory of His coming.

IN HIS EYES IS CLARITY OF VISION

In this repentance and returning to first love, all that has been clamoring for our attention will be silenced and brought to its knees, and ministry will become simple again. This turning is going to bring great clarity to our purpose. The attention is going to move from self-focus and introspection to fixing our gaze on the Lord, and there we will find our clarity of vision.

The Lord is restoring clarity of vision to those who are called to bring His vision to the Church. A mighty move of the Spirit has begun among the Levites and prophets, and it is an invitation to gaze upon Jesus and look into His eyes to find the vision He has for us. This invitation is to deepen the heart of intimacy in these callings. This clarity that is coming to the priests and prophets is vital because they are the ones who have been graced and gifted to minister to the body and reveal what is in the heart of God.

DEALING WITH FEAR AND INSECURITY

I was recently talking with an incredible young leader in this generation. He is truly a man after God's own heart. He was wrestling through the challenges that many leaders walk through around following God obediently and asking me questions while I was washing dishes one night. We were talking about the fear that can come when we are called to step out of the boat and fully trust that God is speaking and that He will be there with us on the water. As we were talking and I was asking him questions, I noticed the cup that I was washing in my hands. I knew the Holy Spirit wanted to say something, so I postured my heart to receive while I continued to listen and wash. The Holy Spirit began to talk to me about how our gifts and personhood can be like that cup—a container to carry His glory and reveal it to the world. The Lord then said something that amazed me. In a vision, He started to show me a picture of a powerful water hose spraying water into the cup. It was first hitting the bottom and filling the cup before it spilled over. I then saw a picture of Jesus removing the bottom of the cup and instead of the cup needing to be filled first, now the water could flow freely through the vessel, still filling it but now the trajectory of the spray went much further. Instantly, the Lord began to speak to my heart about how fear, insecurity, pride, and the need for recognition (which stems from fear) can become a limit on our vessel, forming a cup that has to be filled first before it can be effective. The bottom becomes the limit of how far the water can spray and how many can be affected. When the limit is removed from this vessel, it becomes a conduit instead of a cup.

Immediately, I saw the Lord starting to remove our limits off of us, His people. The Lord in His mercy is releasing a move of His Holy Spirit to uncap us, and He is starting with those called to serve and lead people and to minister to Him in His house. There has been an assignment on these ones to bring distraction and preoccupation with ourselves and limitations, and the Lord is coming to deal with this. This is vital because these are the ones leading us to behold Jesus. If our lenses are unclear, then our leadership will be too.

The Levites in the Old Covenant were not just worshipers, they were also warriors. Our worship is not just an intimate moment, it is an effective warring strategy against the work of the enemy. Our adoration and praise bring us into the reality of

Christ enthroned high above every name and power, and it is from that throne that He releases His authority and establishes His Kingdom here on earth. Jesus's ascension to His throne high above every name, ruler, and principality is vital for us to walk in His authority here on earth.

Worship is the welcome of our hearts, and the heart that worships has eyes to see and behold Jesus for who He is and what He loves. When we see Jesus rightly and know His heart, we are transformed into His likeness and made strong.

The Lord has been after His prophets and priests because like Samuel they have been called as ones to know what is in His heart and soul and gather His people to enter into the knowledge of His glory. They are given the privilege of the invitation to be taken into the chambers of His heart that are not yet revealed to a generation and bring a sound, a song, a melody, or a word that can convey this so that the Bride may enter in. But the gift is only the conduit, not the substance.

The resting of the Holy Spirit is vital to beholding Jesus, and we can only receive it by yielding. This gift is a conduit, but familiarity or pride becomes a cap in our spiritual lives. Corporate worship is a vital part of us entering into the knowledge of Jesus—it is what we were designed to do and what we will do long after our bodies fade on this earth. True worship does not point to anyone or anything else, only to Jesus. We will worship all the days of our lives and into eternity where we will never tire of beholding the Lamb because there will always be a new facet of Him and His glory to enjoy and adore.

This is a move of the Spirit, an awakening of the people of God, which is coming to restore the purity of our worship and words. For us to behold His glory, we must be holy and set apart. Holiness is who God is—He is holy and He cannot be anything else. The word *holy* means to be without spot, with no imperfection, completely set apart. We are called to be holy like God is holy, and He has made every provision for this by the blood of Jesus. The work of the Holy Spirit is to bring conviction to our heart of anything that is not holy and to keep us walking in the light. I see a sweeping wave of the Spirit coming to bring conviction to us, the ones He calls "a royal priesthood and a holy nation," and restore the awe of God to our ministry. We cannot go in intimacy with Jesus where we have no reverence of Him.

HOW DO WE RESPOND?

In the previous chapter, I wrote about an encounter that I had at the airport. The phrase from that encounter that keeps running through my mind as I ponder what God is saying and doing is, "I have asked for much and you have willingly given." Now as much as ever, the right response is to surrender all of who we are and what we have to Jesus, that our lives laid down before Him would be a welcome to the precious Holy Spirit to take a hold of us and drive us deep into the heart of God. It is time that we yield, that we surrender all of our will, mind, and emotions to the purity and perfection of our Lord. We must welcome the work of His Spirit to do what only He can do. It's the cutting off of distractions and anything that is of this world. As my spiritual dad, Bill Johnson, says often, "The world is whatever cools your affections for the Lord." Let us as the Bride respond with intention and complete surrender, willingly giving whatever cools our heart to Him, whatever distracts us from His heart.

I am excited to watch what God does in the Bride in this season. We are in a pivotal time, and we are saying yes to partnering with the Lord in what He is doing and releasing. My prayer for us is that we would be mightily awakened to the power of the Holy Spirit in this hour, that we would become ravenously hungry to know the work of the Spirit, that we would fall in love with the Gospel and truly encounter what it means for the power of Christ to be dwelling within us. I pray that we would come to know the heart of God and long to fulfill what He desires, that Jesus would be glorified and magnified in our life and generation, and that we would walk in deep intimacy with God. Finally, I pray that we would, by His grace, surrender to the work of the Holy Spirit. That we would come to know Him as a Person and our best friend. That we would live a life so dependent on the Spirit of God that we wouldn't know a day without Him moving deeply in our heart's. Let us yield to the ways of the Lord and lay down every hindrance and run this race He has marked our for us. Precious Holy Spirit, come.

As His royal priesthood and holy nation, let us pray the prayer of Romans 12:1 together:

God, we see Your mercy and great love poured out for us, and so we offer ourselves as living sacrifices to You.

May we be holy and pleasing in Your sight. We offer ourselves as worship to You, so that we might walk in Your will and know what is pleasing to You. We know we cannot do this on our own. So, Holy Spirit, we surrender to You and ask You to come fill us and teach us Your ways so that we may know You. Put us on like a glove like You did Gideon, set us ablaze with Your holy fire and burn away anything that hinders us. God, I ask that You ruin us for anything that is not Your presence, that You come and encounter us with the power of Your personhood so that we could never be the same. As You touched me, Holy Spirit, and broke off the fear of man in my life, I pray that You touch every reader by the power of Your Spirit and break every lie that wants to ensnare them. We declare today that the fear of man must die today. We ask You, Holy Spirit, to fill every space and place with Your holy love and clothe us with power as You did the apostles in Acts. Awaken Your Bride, King Jesus, awaken Her to Your beauty, Your worth, and Your majesty. Let Your Church rise up in pure worship of the Lord. We posture ourselves in surrender before You as an altar for Your holy fire, and as we do the Spirit and Bride join together and cry, "Come, Lord Jesus."

Jesus, in Your name we pray this, amen.

ABOUT HAYLEY BRAUN

Hayley Braun is on the Senior Leadership Team of Bethel Church in Redding California and is an Overseer of Bethel School of Supernatural Ministry (BSSM).

Born and raised in Port Elizabeth, South Africa, Hayley moved to Redding to attend BSSM in 2008, where she met her husband Ryan.

Growing up in the church, Hayley discovered her passion early on: the Bride of Christ. She has a deep desire to see the people of God walk in true freedom, living a life liberated by the gospel, in deep intimacy with the Lord, and in connection with one another. Hayley and her family burn for revival and to see the nations encounter God in a real and transformational way. Hayley has spent the last 15 years leading in the Bethel School of Supernatural Ministry in various leadership roles.

Hayley and Ryan have three children and love to spend quality time at home and with their community.